Conflict

En route to

Destiny

Michael L. Jones Sr.

Most Trafford titles are also available at major online book retailers.

Note for Librarians: A cataloguing record for this book is available from Library
and Archives Canada at www.collectionscanada.ca/amicus/index-e.html

Printed in Victoria, BC, Canada.

ISBN: 978-1-4269-1516-1 (sc)

Library of Congress Control Number: 2009934087

*We at Trafford believe that it is the responsibility of us all, as both individuals
and corporations, to make choices that are environmentally and socially sound.
You, in turn, are supporting this responsible conduct each time you purchase a
Trafford book, or make use of our publishing services. To find out how you are
helping, please visit www.trafford.com/responsiblepublishing.html*

*Our mission is to efficiently provide the world's finest, most comprehensive
book publishing service, enabling every author to experience success.
To find out how to publish your book, your way, and have it available
worldwide, visit us online at www.trafford.com*

 www.trafford.com

North America & international
toll-free: 1 888 232 4444 (USA & Canada)
phone: 250 383 6864 ♦ fax: 812 355 4082

Contents

DEDICATION

DEDICATED TO JESUS CHRIST, MY LORD, SAVIOR AND MASTER

TO MY WIFE AND CHILDREN

MARTHA J. JONES, MICHAEL JONES-GARY, MICHAEL WILCOX, TIFFANY JONES, TONY WILLIAMS, SAMUEL JONES AND MICHAEL L. JONES JR.

WITH GRATITUDE

I would like to thank my birth parents (Dorothy J. Palmer-Austin & Terry McArthur Jones) for being used by God to help start me "En route to my Destiny". Inez Sanky and family thank you also for being a part of "destiny". To my friend and fellow- yokes man in the gospel, Michael A. Pouncey, I salute you. Lastly, I want to thank Trafford Publishing for a wonderful job on all of my books to date, "The Making of A Man; My Cross to Bear: "From the Ashes I Rise and "Conflict En Route to Destiny"

MAY GOD BLESS BUTLER COUNTY ALABAMA AND THE ENTIRE STATE OF ALABAMA

Introduction

In life there are always going to be "Conflicts En route to your destiny", but you must learn how to handle those conflicts through the help of Jesus Christ. From the time of my youth up, I never knew that I would have so many conflicts in life, but by the "Grace of God" I made it and so can you.

Please understand that conflicts are actual or perceived opposition of your needs, values and interests. But be sure to identify whether they are internal (within oneself) or external (between two or more individuals). Conflict as a concept can help explain many aspects of your social life, such as social disagreement, conflicts of interests, and fights between individuals, groups, or organizations.

One should not confuse the distinction between the presence and absence of conflict with the difference between competition and co-operation. In competitive situations, the two or more individuals or parties each have mutually inconsistent goals, either party tries to reach their goal it will undermine the attempts of the other to reach theirs. One such example is me and my older brother Jeffery. At times we had our sibling rivalries, while attempting to define who we were. It's just in our competitive nature. Therefore, competitive situations will, by their nature, cause conflict but if you have good sportsmanship or are just fair it won't cause undesirable conflict.

Lastly, remember however, conflict can also occur in cooperative situations, in which two or more individuals or parties have consistent goals, because the manner in which one party tries to reach their goal can still undermine the other individual or party.

A clash of interests, values, actions or directions often sparks a conflict. Conflicts refer to the existence of that clash. Psychologically, a conflict exists when the reduction of one motivating stimulus involves an increase in another, so that a new adjustment is demanded. The word is applicable from the instant that the clash occurs. Even when we say that there is a potential conflict we are implying that there is already a conflict of direction even though a clash may not yet have occurred.

Chapter 1

Conflict; Enroute To Destiny

So what exactly am I saying to you when I say, "Conflict, En route to Destiny"? If you stayed tuned, I promise you will find out. But first one must understand what conflict is and is not. When a person does an in-depth study of conflict what does he or she find? There are several areas within one's life that conflict can play a part in. One area deals with an interpersonal level Interpersonal conflict requires at least two people. With this form of conflict there may be a conflict within one's self, or an intrapersonal conflict; both which are generally studied by psychologists.

Follow me for a moment as I attempt to relate to you, the definition of conflict. Conflict inherently involves some sense of struggle or incompatibility or perceived difference among values, goals, or desires. It also deals with actions, whether overt or covert, which are key to interpersonal conflict. Until the action or expression occurs, conflict is latent, meaning that it is lurking below the surface.

The problem or conflict comes when there are powers or attempts made to influence a person to do or don't do a particular thing. This is inevitably what occurs within the person that causes conflicts within their lives.

On the other hand, if the parties really don't care about the outcome, the discussion probably doesn't rise to the level where it can be called a conflict. When people argue without caring about what happens next or without a sense of involvement and struggle, it probably is just a disagreement, and not a conflict.

Conflict is not a breakdown in communication, but a process that is ongoing. The communication process is not like a car that can break or cease to function. Conflict involves discussing what the disagreements is all about.

Conflict is not based on whether a situation is good or bad. Although some people may tend to remember only the conflicts that were painful, conflict itself is a normal part of being human. Harmony is neither normal nor necessarily desirable as a permanent state of being. It is normal in relationships for differences to occur occasionally, just as it is normal in businesses for changes in goals and directions to occur. What we have to remember is that "conflict" is normal. Conflict is also not automatically resolved by communication. Managing conflicts productively is a skill.

There was a time in my life where I was introduced to conflict at different levels. There were some that I was able to handle on my own and there were others conflict situations where I needed some assistance. But don't be ashamed or dismayed if you're unable to handle every conflict situation that arises within your life. Remember, "managing conflicts productively is a skill".

One key nugget that I have to offer you, the reader, is that conflict resolution implies that conflicts can be resolved--finished, completed, overcome, or permanently settled. The label conflict management was intentionally chosen by communication scholars because the term evokes a process view of the choices and behaviors that come into play during conflicts.

Communication during conflict requires both choice and action-- actions that may or may not solve the conflict permanently. The term conflict management implies that conflict is not an "on" or "off" phenomenon. Some conflicts are enduring and the best we can hope for is to manage the level and manifestation of conflict--to sustain a good working relationship free from negative behaviors or violence. Communication scholars generally agree that conflict: is a process, that is inevitable, but it also is a normal part of life. After reading this paragraph, it is my hope that you will be able to continue through the rest of this section and learn more about the nature of conflict.

How do you define conflict? What is conflict really? There are so many definitions and assumptions concerning the term conflict that it's hard to know what to believe. Some people may define conflict as a disagreement through which the parties involved perceive a threat to their needs, interests or concerns. Within this simple definition there are several important understandings that must emerge from within this particular definition or train of thought.

Let's first look at the word disagreement. When we say disagreement, generally, we are aware there is some level of difference in the positions of the two (or more) parties involved in the conflict. But the true disagreement versus the perceived disagreement may be quite different from one another. In fact, conflict tends to be accompanied by significant levels of misunderstanding that exaggerate the perceived disagreement considerably. If we can understand the true areas of disagreement, this will help us solve the right problems and manage the true needs of the parties.

Then the definition states that there parties of people involved. What we need to understand is that there are often disparities in our sense of who is involved in the conflict. Sometimes, people are surprised to learn they are a party to the conflict, while other times we are shocked to learn we are not included in the disagreement.

On many occasions, people who are seen as part of the social system (e.g., work team, family, company) are influenced to participate in the dispute, whether they would personally define the situation in that way or not. In the above example, people very readily "take sides" based upon current perceptions of the issues, past issues and relationships, roles within the organization, and other factors. The parties involved can become an elusive concept to define.

But the part that we should pay closet attention to is the perceived threat. You see, people may respond to the perceived threat, rather than the true threat, facing them. So, while the perception doesn't become reality per se, people's behaviors, feelings and ongoing responses become modified by that evolving sense of the threat they confront. If we can work to understand the true threat (issues) and develop strategies (solutions) that manage it (agreement), we are acting constructively to manage the conflict.

Wherever we see conflict, I guarantee you will notice that there is a need, interests or concern that needs to be addressed. There is a tendency to narrowly define "the problem" as one of substance, task, and near-term viability. However, workplace conflicts tend to be far more complex than that, for they involve ongoing relationships with complex, emotional components.

Simply stated, there are always procedural needs and psychological needs to be addressed within the conflict, in addition to the substantive needs that are generally presented. And the durability of the interests and concerns of the parties transcends the immediate presenting situation. Any efforts to resolve conflicts effectively must take these points into account.

So, is it still a simple definition of conflict? We think so, but we must respect that within its elegant simplicity lies a complex set of issues to address. Therefore, it is not surprising that satisfactory resolution of most conflicts can prove so challenging and time consuming to address.

We also need to accept the fact that conflicts most often occur when people (or other parties) perceive that, as a consequence of a disagreement, there is a threat to their needs, interests or concerns. Although conflict is a normal part of organization life, providing numerous opportunities for growth through improved understanding and insight, there is a tendency to view conflict as a negative experience caused by abnormally difficult circumstances.

Those participants within the conflict environment tend to perceive limited options and finite resources available in seeking solutions, rather than multiple possibilities that may exist 'outside the box' in which we are problem-solving.

Here are a few points which are worth reiterating before proceeding further in this book:

- A conflict is more than a mere disagreement - it is a situation in which people perceive a threat (physical, emotional, power, status, etc.) to their well-being. As such, it is a meaningful experience in people's lives, not to be shrugged off by a mere, "it will pass..."

- Participants in conflicts tend to respond on the basis of their perceptions of the situation, rather than an objective review of it. As such, people filter their perceptions (and reactions) through their values, culture, beliefs, information, experience, gender, and other variables. Conflict responses are both filled with ideas and feelings that can be very strong and powerful guides to our sense of possible solutions.

- As in any problem, conflicts contain substantive, procedural, and psychological dimensions to be negotiated. In order to best understand the threat perceived by those engaged in a conflict, we need to consider all of these dimensions.

- Conflicts are normal experiences within the work environment. They are also, to a large degree, predictable and expectable situations that naturally arise as we go about managing complex and stressful projects in which we are significantly invested. As such, if we develop procedures for identifying conflicts likely to arise, as well as systems through which we can constructively manage conflicts, we may be able to discover new opportunities to transform conflict into a productive learning experience.

- Creative problem-solving strategies are essential to positive approaches to conflict management. We need to transform the situation from one in which it is 'my way or the highway' into one in which we entertain new possibilities that have been otherwise elusive.

As a behavioral analysis student I had to learn more about this process called "Conflict". I had to examine my own self in order to see how I would respond to Conflict: you know my thoughts, feelings, and my physical responses; from the behavioral aspect.

In addition to the behavioral responses that were summarized in some of my textbooks, which dealt with the various conflict styles that we have such as emotional, cognitive and physical responses to conflict. These were important windows into our experience, during in which conflict frequently told me more about what is the true source of my threat that I perceived. By understanding my thoughts, feelings and physical responses to conflict, I may get better insights into the best potential solutions to my situation. There are two responses that I would like to elaborate on which are emotional, cognitive and physical responses.

- **Emotional responses:** These are the feelings we experience in conflict, ranging from anger and fear to despair and confusion. Emotional responses are often misunderstood, as people tend to believe that others feel the same as they do. Thus, differing emotional responses are confusing and, at times, threatening.

- **Cognitive responses:** These are our ideas and thoughts about a conflict, often present as inner voices or internal observers in the midst of a situation. Through sub-vocalization (i.e., self-talk), we come to understand these cognitive responses. For example, we might think any of the following things in response to another person taking a parking spot just as we are ready to park:

- "That jerk! Who does he think he is! What a sense of entitlement!"

or:

   "I wonder if he realizes what he has done. He seems
   lost in his own thoughts. I hope he is okay."

or:

   "What am I supposed to do? Now I'm going to be late
   for my meeting… Should I say something to him?
   What if he gets mad at me?"

Such differing cognitive responses contribute to emotional and behavioral responses, where self-talk can either promote a positive or negative feedback loop in the situation.

- **Physical responses:** These responses can play an important role in our ability to meet our needs in the conflict. They include heightened stress, bodily tension, increased perspiration, tunnel vision, shallow or accelerated breathing, nausea, and rapid heartbeat. These responses are similar to those we experience in high-anxiety situations, and they may be managed through stress management techniques. Establishing a calmer environment in which emotions can be managed is more likely if the physical response is addressed effectively.

I hope that you, the reader have received a bit more information concerning your perceived idea of what a conflict is or isn't. I also hope that you will be better able to handle or seek help during those times in which a conflict could probably get out of control. I pray this information will aid you in better handling "Conflict, while you're enroute to your destiny". It is also my desire that you also better understand the three types of responses to conflict which were emotional, cognitive and physical.

As I begin to close this portion of the introduction, it is my sincere hopes that I can also aid you in understanding the role of perception in conflicts. The Role of Perceptions in "Conflict" as noted in the basic definition of conflict, describes to us that conflict is a disagreement through which the parties involved perceive a threat to their needs, interests or concerns. One key element of this definition is the idea that each party may have a different perception of any given situation. We can anticipate having such differences due to a number of factors that create "perceptual filters" that influence our responses to the situation:

- **Culture, race, and ethnicity:** Our varying cultural backgrounds influence us to hold certain beliefs about the social structure of our world, as well as the role of conflict in that experience. We may have learned to value substantive, procedural and psychological needs differently as a result, thus influencing our willingness to engage in various modes of negotiation and efforts to manage the conflict

- **Gender and sexuality:** Men and women often perceive situations somewhat differently, based on both their experiences in the world (which relates to power and privilege, as do race and ethnicity) and socialization patterns that reinforce the importance of relationships vs. task, substance vs. process, immediacy vs. long-term outcomes. As a result, men and women will often approach conflictive situations

7

with differing mindsets about the desired outcomes from the situation, as well as the set of possible solutions that may exist.

- **Knowledge (general and situational):** Parties respond to given conflicts on the basis of the knowledge they may have about the issue at hand. This includes situation-specific knowledge (i.e., "Do I understand what is going on here?") and general knowledge (i.e., "Have I experienced this type of situation before?" or "Have I studied about similar situations before?"). Such information can influence the person's willingness to engage in efforts to manage the conflict, either reinforcing confidence to deal with the dilemma or undermining one's willingness to flexibly consider alternatives.

- **Impressions of the Messenger:** If the person sharing the message - the messenger - is perceived to be a threat (powerful, scary, unknown, etc.), this can influence our responses to the overall situation being experienced. For example, if a big scary-looking guy is approaching me rapidly, yelling "Get out of the way!" I may respond differently than if a diminutive, calm person would express the same message to me. As well, if I knew either one of them previously, I might respond differently based upon that prior sense of their credibility: I am more inclined to listen with respect to someone I view as credible than if the message comes from someone who lacks credibility and integrity in my mind.

- **Previous experiences:** Some of us have had profound, significant life experiences that continue to influence our perceptions of current situations. These experiences may have left us fearful, lacking trust, and reluctant to take risks. On the other hand, previous experiences may have left us confident, willing to take chances and experience the unknown. Either way, we must acknowledge the role of previous experiences as elements of our perceptual filter in the current dilemma.

Please understand that these factors (along with others) conspire to form the perceptual filters through which we experience conflict. As a result, our reactions to the threat and dilemma posed by conflict should be anticipated to include varying understandings of the situation. This also means that we can anticipate that in many conflicts there will be significant misunderstanding of each other's perceptions, needs and feelings. These challenges contribute to our emerging sense, during conflict, that the situation is overwhelming and unsolvable. As such, they become critical sources of potential understanding, insight and possibility.

Chapter 2

Jeremiah 29:11

"For I know the thoughts that I think toward you, saith the LORD, thoughts of peace, and not of evil, to give you an expected end."

"For I know the plans I have for you," declares the LORD, "plans to prosper you and not to harm you, plans to give you hope and a future." (NIV version)

So you ask, why this verse? This very well may be the verse that will have the most special meaning to you. It has a powerful message and it may be very instrumental in your decision to accept Christ into your life. Do you understand that you will run into "Conflict" while you're "En route to your Destiny".

So you want to know what is the meaning of this particular verse, huh?

For many years, you may have taken the words in the verse at face value. It may not be until you heard someone questioning the meaning that you may decide to do some research of for yourself. You may have found quite a few blogs and sermons⸢ pertaining to the context and true meaning of this particular verse.

It is important, imperative actually, that we understand the context of passages from the Bible. In studying the context of Jeremiah 29:11, I feel I have a better understanding of the true meaning. Even if you omit the contextualized words "plans to prosper you and not to harm you", I believe this verse still has a very powerful message: God knows us personally, and He has a plan for us, and allows us to find hope in Him. It is good for us to understand that this verse was given as advice to the captives in Babylon. I want to go briefly back to verse 8 and then continue forward to verse 11.

Jeremiah 29:8-11

8 For thus saith the LORD of hosts, the God of Israel; Let not your prophets and your diviners, that be in the midst of you, deceive you, neither hearken to your dreams which ye cause to be dreamed.

9 For they prophesy falsely unto you in my name: I have not sent them, saith the LORD.

10 For thus saith the LORD, That after seventy years be accomplished at Babylon I will visit you, and perform my good word toward you, in causing you to return to this place.

11 For I know the thoughts that I think toward you, saith the LORD, thoughts of peace, and not of evil, to give you an expected end.

These verses of scripture were given to help make the people quiet and easy while they were in their captivity. The first thing that we have to look at is that God takes them off from building upon the false foundation which their pretended prophets laid. They told them that their captivity should be short, and therefore that they must not think of taking root in Babylon, but be upon the wing to go back; "Now herein they deceive you," says God; "they prophesy a lie to you, though they prophesy in my name. But let them not deceive you, suffer not yourselves to be deluded by them.

What they had to remember was that as long as they have the Word of Truth to try the spirits by the spirit, then it would be their fault they

11

were deceived. It will be by the Word of Truth that they would be made to be undeceived, if you mind me using that form of language.

According to the Matthew Henry Commentary, God continues to tell them "Hearken not to your dreams, which you cause to be dreamed. He means either the dreams or fancies which the people pleased themselves with, and with which they filled their own heads (by thinking and speaking of nothing else but a speedy enlargement when they were awake they caused themselves to dream of in their vain expectations), or even the dreams which the prophets dreamed and grounded their prophecies on.

God tells the people, They are your dreams, because they pleased them, and also because they were the dreams that they desired and wished for. They caused them to be dreamed because the people were willing to listen and except them as being so. They were the dreams of their own bespeaking. False prophets would not flatter people in their sins, but they that loved to be flattered, and smoothly spoken to by those false prophets.

God gives them a good foundation to build their hopes on. We would not persuade people to pull down the house they have built upon the sand, but that there is a rock ready for them to rebuild upon. God here promises them that, tough they should not return quickly, they should return at length, after seventy years be accomplished.

By this, it appears that the seventy years of captivity are not to be reckoned form the last captivity, but the first. Note, though the deliverance of the church does not come in our time, it is sufficient that it will come in God's time, and we are sure that that is the best time. The promise is that God will visit them in mercy; though He had long seemed to be strange to them, he will come among them and appear for them, and put honor upon them, as great men do upon their inferiors by coming to visit them.

He, meaning God, will put an end to their captivity, and turn away all the calamities of it. Though they are dispersed, some in one country and some in another, He will gather them form all the places whither they are driven. He will set up a standard for them all to resort to, and incorporate them again in one body. And though they are at a great distance they shall by bought again to their own land, to the place whence they were carried captive.

Now this shall be the performance of God's promise to them: will perform my good word towards you. Let not the falling of those predictions which are delivered as from God lessen the reputation of those that really are from Him. That which is indeed God's Word is a good Word, and therefore iot will be made good, and not one iota or tittle of it shall fall to the ground. "Hath he said, and shall He not do it?" This will make their return out of captivity very comfortable, that it will be the performance of God's goo Word to them, the product of a gracious promise.

Next, we should see that this shall be done in pursuance of God's purposes concerning them; the children of Israel. Listen again at what God is saying to them, "I know the thoughts that I think towards you. Known unto God are all his works, for known unto Him are all His thoughts (Acts 15:18) and his works agree exactly with His thoughts. He does all things according to the counsel of His will.

You see, we often do not know our own thoughts, nor do we know our own mind, but God is never at any uncertainty within Himself. We are sometimes ready to fear that God's designs concerning us are all against us, but he knows the contrary concerning His own people; that they are all working towards the expected end, which e will give in due time.

The end they expect will come, though perhaps not when they expect it. He wants us to have patience till the fruit is ripe, and then we shall have it. He will give us an end, and an expectation of fullfilment. He will give us to see the end (the comfortable termination) of our trouble, although it seems to have lasted a long time, it still shall not last always.

I'm trying to get us to picture the time of Zion's favor, yes, the set time will come. When things are at the worst we will begin to mend; it is then that He will give us to see the glorious perfection of our deliveranc; for, as for God, His Work is perfect. Always remember that He that in the beginning finished the heavens and the earth, and all the hosts of both, will finish all the blessings of both to his people.

When He begins in ways of mercy He will make an end. God does nothing half way. He will give us to see the ecpectation, that end which we desire and hope for, and He also understands that we have been longing for it for a while. He will give us, not the expectations of fears, nor the expectations of our fancies, but the expectations of our faith, and the end which He has promised because it will turn out for our best.

This shall be in answer to our prayers and supplications to God (Jeremiah 29:12-15). God will stir us up to pray: Then shall you call upon me, and you you shall go, and pray unto me. Note, When God is about to give His people the epected good He pours out a spirit of prayer, and it is a good sign that He is coming towards us in mercy. Then, when we see the expected end approaching, we shall call upon Him.

Understand this also, promises are given, not to supercede, but to quicken and encourage prayer. When deliverance is coming we must by prayer go forth to meet it. When Daniel understood that the 70 years were near expiring, then he set his face with more fervency than ever to seek the Lord (Daniel 9:2-3).

He, meaning God, will stir up Himself to come and save us (Psalms 80:2): I will hearken unto you, and I will be found of you. God has said it, and we may depend upon it. Seek and you shall find Him, meaning God. We have a general rule laid down: You shall find me when ou shall search for me with all your heart. In seeking God we must seach for Him. We must accomplish a diligent search, because we are searching for directions during the process of seeking Him. We are searching for the encouragements which will aide in our faith and hope. We must continue seeking, and be willing to endure the pains in seeking God during our search. This is what we must do with our heart (that is, in sincerity and uprightness), and with our whole heart (that is, with vigor and fervency, putting forth all tha is within us in prayer), and those who still seek God shall find Him, and not only that, shall find in Him our bountiful rewarder. God never ever told us to seek Him in vain.

Before I conclude this chapter, I want to share a bit of life as it pertains to my "destiny" in Jesus Christ. This information can be also found in my first book entitled "The Making of A Man; My Cross to Bear", in the first chapter of that book. The chapter is entitled, "How did I get to this point in my life". In other words, I did I get to this point of my "destiny" for which God controls. It reads:

Oftentimes throughout my adult life I wondered why I was put here on earth. Feelings of despair, depression, confused and unnerved by my children, I look for answers from above. It seems as though there is no answer to be found. There are people in the world that feel just like me. I long for the assurance that God would smile and move towards me, but I assumed that He might be too selective to feel anything for me. I may even see Him as an unchanging, eternal spirit who lives far above the ever-changing winds of pain and emotion that blow in and out of my lives.

But that is not true of the God of the Bible. The Scriptures assures all road worn, dejected people, and everyone else, that He feels deeply for the most broken. He cannot be touched by our strengths, but only by our weaknesses. While God's character never changes, His affections do change. To know God is to affect Him. While God knew us, loved us, and chose us along with all His people in eternity past (Ephesians 1:3-6), He relates to us personally and presently in a very intimate way. He rejoices with us when we are happy, sorrows when we are sad, and grieves when we are bad. He has made Himself just that vulnerable to us. He has exposed His own heart to all of the loveless and heartless things that we do to Him. The Bible tells us that God can be:

- Pleased (Hebrews 11:5)
- Grieved and sorrowful (Genesis 6:6;Ephesians 4:30-32).
- Provoked and tested (Psalms 78:40-41).
- Burdened and wearied (Isaiah 43:24).
- Angered, agitated, and furious (Ezekiel 16:42-43).

Specifically, Ephesians 4:30-32 says, "Do not grieve the Holy Spirit of God, by whom you were sealed for the day of redemption. Let all bitterness, wrath, anger, clamor, and evil speaking be put away from you, with all malice. And be kind to one another, tenderhearted, forgiving one another, just as God in Christ forgave you."

The greatest evidence of His decision to make Himself vulnerable to us is found in the personal pains and sorrows of The One who with His own mind and heart revealed the Father to us. In the face of Jesus Christ, we find the face of God. He is the One who suffered for us so He could bring us to the Father. He loves us that much! It might be hard for us to personalize that kind of love when we know we are only one in a world of more than 5 billion people.

But we need to keep in mind that it is we in which we are talking about. God does not have our limitations. He is not confined to human, one-at-a-time relationships.

Rather, the One who made the world is able to relate intimately to as many of us at the same time as He desires. How do we know God has that kind of capacity? We might come to that conclusion by reflecting on the size and complexity of the universe He created. Or we might consider the vast amounts of knowledge and information that finite people like ourselves can amass through the global Internet. Or we might simply trust the words of the One who said:

Are not two sparrows sold for a copper coin? And not one of them falls to the ground apart from your Father's will. But the very hairs of our head is also counting the tears, the moments of our fears, and the depth of the swirling waters threatening to engulf us.

If God knows us with this kind of knowledge, then we are never as alone as we feel. We are need without help. We are never out of the Father's reach. Even though He might test our faith and our patience by not responding immediately in the way we want Him to, we can be are assured with a peace and confidence that can calm the turbulence within and lead to dramatic changes in us. To know God is to be affected by Him. Think for a moment about the people who have changed your life for the better. Maybe it was the teacher who inspired you to go for your dreams. Maybe it was the parent or grandparent whose words and hugs made you feel deeply loved. Maybe it was the neighbor who showed you by his example that any job worth having is worth doing well. Looking back, you can see that knowing these people changed your life.

What is true of these people will be even more of those who come to know God. No one can know Him without being changed by Him. Anyone who comes into God's presence will be touched and changed by the One who loves us enough to accept us as we are, but loves us too much to leave us that way. The apostle James described such a personal relationship with God like this:

Therefore submit to God. Resist the devil and he will flee from you. Draw near to God and He will draw near to you. Cleanse your hands, you sinners; and purify your hearts, you double-minded. Lament and mourn and weep! Let your laughter be turned to mourning and your joy to gloom. Humble yourselves in the sight of the Lord, and He will lift you up (4:7-10).

To know of God in this way means allowing our hearts to be broken by the things that break His heart. It means finding joy in the things that bring Him joy, discovering strength in His strength, and receiving hope in the assurance that nothing is too hard for him. It means finding a new lease on life in One who offers us forgiveness in exchange for our repentance, comfort in trade for our sorrow, and the promise of a world to come for our willingness to release our grip on this present one. We are changed as we discover that to know God is to love Him. To love Him is to give Him first place in our hearts. Giving Him first place is to care about those He cares about, to love what He loves, to hate what He hates, and to join Him in the family business of redeeming broken lives. This is the kind of healthy relationship that God calls us to.

But such maturity doesn't just happen. Sometimes a personal relationship with God remains a faint glimmer of what it was meant to be. Sometimes we stop short of the growth to which God call us. Years ago, I had a pastor who spoke a word to me, while praying for me, that I would have the "Spirit of Job'. I didn't know much about Job, I was just glad to hear a Word from God, because I was wondering if I was put here on Earth just to suffer. What I did know was that in the end that Job was a successful and blessed man of God. I didn't get a full realization of all that he endured to reach the point of success; he suffered tremendously. The book of Job does discuss his ups and downs, i.e. dealing with his children, wife, and his doubtful friends, but through it all he remained faithful to God, unlike me. As an adult, I look back over my life and wonder what happened in my life to get me to the point where I am today. Was it the sickness that I endured as a baby? No, because the only part of that I remember is actually being rushed to the hospital and being put in an incubator around the age of 1 to 2 years of age. I could remember that vision as if it were yesterday. I remember being with my great grandmother in the projects in Alabama crawling up the sidewalk outside, and even the day she died. It was only that small glimpse of my childhood that I could remember, up to the ages of 3 or 4 years.

Even when you or I can't remember the past, it shouldn't prevent us from living now, and shouldn't stop us from pressing towards the mark of the prize of the high calling of God in Christ Jesus. But before I could move on in life, I had to deal with some issues; the enemy within.

Within me laid a desire to have a virgin. The desire to be someone's first sexual partner seemed to be of the uttermost importance. This desire within me was not of God, but could only be delivered from within me, by God. If I wanted to be free, I had to be willing to challenge all the definitions of my masculinity. I had to fight against many of the things that most men would rather forget. Freedom would only come when I challenged myself; when I opened up and said things to myself that I might not have admitted to my wife, to my friends, or to my parents. It was time for me to confront the old issues in my life. These issues were the enemy of my soul. The book of Romans 1:21-28, painted a scary picture of men who failed to deal with their enemy within themselves:

21 Because that, when they knew God, they glorified him not as God, neither were thankful; but became vain in their imaginations, and their foolish heart was darkened.

22 Professing themselves to be wise, they became fools,

23 And changed the glory of the uncorruptible God into an image made like to corruptible man, and to birds, and four-footed beasts, and creeping things

24 Wherefore God also gave them up to uncleanness through the lusts of their own hearts, to dishonour their own bodies between themselves:

25 Who changed the truth of God into a lie, and worshipped and served the creature more than the Creator, who is blessed for ever. Amen.

26 For this cause God gave them up unto vile affections: for even their women did change the natural use into that which is against nature;

27 And likewise also the men, leaving the natural use of the woman, burned in their lust one toward another; men with men working that which is unseemly and receiving in themselves that recompense of their error which was meet.

28 And even as they did not like to retain God in their knowledge, God gave them over to a reprobate mind, to do those things which are not convenient...

These people may or may not have once known the Lord, but they decided not to glorify Him as God. His judgment was to turn them over to themselves! When we are left to our own selves, we may be surprised to know how corrupt we really are or can be. We may hide many things in us that we don't talk about. There are hidden things in us that we look down on others for, but we make sure that no one knows what is really on the inside of our heart. We know the evil that is lurking in the dark corners of our heart. The scary thing is that you never know when these things are going to rise up within us. When the right button is pushed, it allows your enemy within you to rear its ugly head. You may find yourself doing or wanting to do things that you felt you could never even have thought of. Because you don't fully understand how many moral or emotional landmines are buried inside you, you may be vulnerable to erupt at any moment.

The greatest and most lethal weapon that the enemy can ever challenged us with is ourselves. We are challenged in unique and special ways to help us to know who we are, despite our handicaps. When we don't have goals, it is easy for others to impose on us their ideas of who we are and are not, and of what we should and should not be doing.

Anytime we don't know and understand our purpose, or who we were created to be, we become vulnerable to manipulation. If you are not careful, you could have ended up like me, feeling that the power of God was unable or unwilling to change my situation. Here's a word of encouragement, found in the book of Romans 4:17, part b:

17 God "calleth those things which be not as though they were".

Why? He knows He has the power to make me become what He says I will be. He is not afraid to call me holy and blameless, even while

I am I am still confused, in trouble and turmoil! I may have been guilty of inflicting domestic violence or mental abuse, but God says, "When I get through with him, he's going to be a deacon in the church, and I did become one". He didn't stop there; he made me a preacher, Praise God. I thank Him for blessing me and keeping me when I was in MY mess.

God has reserved a place for me, and "there isn't anyone who will be able to get in that place but me". Some of my enemies and friends thought that I wouldn't be there, but God said it will and is so; to the Glory of God. There were times when even I thought that I wouldn't be there. God had to get me ready. I had to get ready before I could be in the place that God had for me. He has reserved a place for me. When I was in my darkest sin, God had His angels watching over me. When I may have wanted to slap my wife around and boasted about how I wasn't going to church, or preach God's Word again, God protected me from myself. He knew exactly how He was going to pull that bitterness out of me and bring me to my knees. I am a miracle. God allowed me to share that message in Kuwait, "Looking at a Miracle", on New Years Eve. 2002.

If God had dealt with me according to my sins, I would be dead. But God is merciful. He was determined to turn me around and place in a position where he could minister to me. Because I belong to God, He went to extreme measures to get me away from people, the cliques and clubs, bars, society and any other kind of entanglement that would have hindered me from hearing His voice. But when I decided to listen, when He called, he arranged things in my life so He could have me to Himself completely. Because of God's Love and determination in my life, I was then able to "Walk in Destiny" as I faced the "Conflicts" of life.

Chapter 3

God Reveals Himself

Whenever God has a plan for your life, He will first reveal Himself to you or I. What am I saying? God will make known (something hidden or kept secret). He will disclose or divulge the thing that He was you to know or do. He will expose it to you in order for you to be able to view it. In theological terms it means that He will make it known by supernatural or divine means.

As I begun to think on the title of this book, one of the first persons I could think of was Moses. As we take a look at Moses' life and we will see that he endured much "conflict in route to his destiny". Let's start by looking at how Moses' became Moses. Remember this will only be a quick snap shot of his life for right now.

Moses was born between 1300 and 1150 B.C., in Egypt. He died between 1300 and 1150 B.C. (by God's decree), and he is best known as the Hebrew liberator who received the Ten Commandments. Moses birth name at birth was "Moshe". Moses was the most important figure in Judaism. Moses parted the Red Sea to free his people and brought them the Ten Commandments on stone tablets. His story appears early in the Bible and is filled with miracles and talks with God.

At his birth, the Hebrews, descendants of Abraham, Isaac and Jacob (Israel), are slaves to Egypt's king (Pharaoh) who has ordered newborn males killed. Moses' mother hides him in a papyrus basket among the Nile's reeds; Pharaoh's daughter finds him, takes pity and adopts him. He flees as a young man, but God appears to him in a burning bush years later and sends him back with his brother, Aaron, to demand the Israelites' release. Plagues arrive, the Hebrews escape, and Egypt's army drowns in the Red Sea.

A wilderness sojourn follows, in which God, through Moses, makes a covenant with the Hebrews and lays out rites of worship and laws of communal and personal behavior. At age 120, Moses dies by God's decree just before the people enter the land known in recent centuries as Palestine and Israel.

His Hebrew name, Moshe, means "the one who draws out"... His story starts in Exodus and ends in Deuteronomy, two of the "five books of Moses" or, in Hebrew, the Torah ("law"). It includes the first Passover, just before the escape from Egypt... The burning bush and stone tablets appear on Mt. Sinai. Its precise location on the Sinai Peninsula is uncertain... Moses is also a figure of faith in Christianity and a prophet in Islam; the Koran's account is similar to the Bible's but less detailed.

THE BIRTH OF MOSES

Follow me as I take you on a journey concerning the birth of "Moses". This journey will start in the Exodus 2:1-4.

Exodus 2:1-4

1 And there went a man of the house of Levi, and took to wife a daughter of Levi.
2 And the woman conceived, and bare a son: and when she saw him that he was a goodly child, she hid him three months.

3 And when she could not longer hide him, she took for him an ark of bulrushes, and daubed it with slime and with pitch, and put the child therein; and she laid it in the flags by the river's brink.

4 And his sister stood afar off, to wit what would be done to him.

This means that Moses was a member of the Tribe of Levi, which were to be the Priestly Tribe. He was a Type of Christ, our Great High Priest. Miriam and Aaron, Moses' sister and brother, were already born when Moses was born. Jochebed was his mother, with Amram being his father.

When we look at Moses, one could say, not me, "From Adam to Christ there is none greater than Moses. He was one of the few characters found within the scriptures whose course was sketched from this infancy to his death. In other words, his conflict, along with his destiny was already laid out. The fierce light of criticism, concerning Moses' life, has been turned upon him for generations, but he is still one of the most commanding figures of the ancient world.

In character, and faith, in the uniqueness of his position assigned him as mediator of the Old Covenant, and also in the achievements that he accomplished through God, he stands favorably first among the heroes of the Old Testament. All of God's early dealings with Israel were transacted through Moses. He was a Prophet, Priest, and King in one person, and so united all the great and important functions which later were distributed among a plurality of persons. The history of such an one is worthy of the strictest attention, and his remarkable life deserves the closet study.

We will see how Pharaoh's orders disallowed the mother of Moses to keep her child under her terms. Pharoah had given the orders that all boy babies were to be instantly killed. But watch God and see how He not only controlled Moses' destiny, but yours and mine as well. I want you to see that which stands out so vividly in this account. This thing that stood out so much was the faith of Jochedbed, the mother of Moses. She no doubt believed and was led by the moment of the Lord. You see in verse three of chapter one of Exodus, she was led to put Moses in in an ark of bulrushes, daubed in slime and pitch, and placed at the river's brink. No one could have controlled this situation better than God Himself. Do you see the 1st line of "conflict" that was introduced to Moses as he journeyed his way to his "destiny"?

MOSES EARLY YEARS

How many of us really remember all that has taken places in the early stages of our life. Although you may not, it is imperative that you do. For in order to get where you are going it is important to understand where you came from. You, the reader, may be able to better understand the direction that I am taking you, as you follow me as I continue to discuss Moses' life throughout this chapter. His life resembles all of our lives because he faced, "Conflict en route to his destiny", as we will do in our life time. Exodus 2:5-10 reads:

5 And the daughter of Pharaoh came down to wash herself at the river; and her maidens walked along by the river's side; and when she saw the ark among the flags, she sent her maid to fetch it.

6 And when she had opened it, she saw the child: and, behold, the babe wept. And she had compassion on him, and said, This is one of the Hebrews' children.

7 Then said his sister to Pharaoh's daughter, Shall I go and call to thee a nurse of the Hebrew women, that she may nurse the child for thee?

8 And Pharaoh's daughter said to her, Go. And the maid went and called the child's mother.

9 And Pharaoh's daughter said unto her, Take this child away, and nurse it for me, and I will give thee thy wages. And the women took the child, and nursed it.

10 And the child grew, and she brought him unto Pharaoh's daughter, and he became her son. And she called his name Moses: and she said, Because I drew him out of the water.

As we continue with Moses' life story, I want you to be encouraged with the fact of knowing that God is not a respecter of persons. What He has done for others, He is willing to do for you. The difference is that you have to be in line with His movement. You also have to be willing and obedient to His call on your life. Look at how great God is at what He does. The Lord had something in mind that Jochedbed could not have possibly dreamed. When she went to put Moses at the brink of the river, the Holy Spirit had everything timed just right: the place, the person, and the progress. This is why we all should be encouraged. Look at the movement of God.

The scriptures go on to say that the daughter of Pharaoh had opened the basket, and saw the child, Moses cried. But watch God, Moses' sister asked Pharaoh's daughter, "Shall I go and call to thee a nurse of the Hebrew women, that she may nurse the child for thee?" And Pharaoh's daughter said to her, Go. And the maid went and called the child's mother. We have to understand that Miriam couldn't have done this on her own, for she was led by the Lord.

Only God could have had Moses placed in the right place, for the right person to see him at the right time. Will you allow God to do the same for you. I would like you to remember this saying, "***On that memorable day, God floated His navy on the tears of a baby's cheek***".

I need you to catch this next statement. At the time that Pharoah's daughter permitted Miriam to go and bring back a nurse, she did know that the nurse would be Moses' mother, Jochebed. So Jochebed would then take care of baby Moses, and be paid by the State for doing what a true mother wants to do anyway. I now Satan wasn't happy about the outcome of Moses "early years of life".

Jochebed had to understand that at any given time, the daughter of Pharaoh could wand Moses to come to live with her in the Palace. So at the beckoning of her call, Moses then was raised to be of Pharaoh's house in Egypt. To show you how much the Holy Spirit thought of the palace of Pharaoh, He, in effect devoted only one Verse to these years of Moses' life. Now we need to speed ahead to the point of God's getting Moses' attention.

GOD GETS MOSES' ATTENTION AND REVEALS HIMSELF TO MOSES

Forty years had passed since Moses had fled Egypt (Acts 7:30). Pharaoh wanted Moses' life in return for the Egyptian that he had killed. After meeting Jethro in the land of Midian and marrying one of his daughters, Moses tended sheep for his father-in-law for many years. As he wandered in the desert near Mount Horeb, he might have thought that God had forgotten about him and the Hebrews in bondage in Egypt.

The angel who appeared to Moses was no ordinary angel. In the Old Testament, the term "angel of the Lord" (Exodus 3:2) may have indicated an appearance of Christ Himself before His birth in Bethlehem. Here Moses saw the angel in a fire that did not devour the bush it was burning. Such a sight was sure to get Moses' attention, and it did.

I want to briefly give you a description of the burning bush. I was blessed to go to Israel and see the alleged location of the "burning bush" in 1990, as I was part of a "Peace keeping Tour in Egypt. The burning bush is an object described by the Book of Exodus as being located on Mount Horeb; according to the narrative, the bush was on fire, but was not consumed by the flames, hence the name. In the narrative, the burning bush is the location at which Moses was appointed by God to lead the Israelites out of Egypt and into Canaan.

The Hebrew word used in the narrative, that is translated into English as bush, is seneh (XXX), which refers in particular to brambles seneh is a biblical dis legomenon, only appearing in two places, both of which describe the burning bush. It is possible that the reference to a burning bush is based on a mistaken interpretation of Sinai (XXXX), a mountain described by the Bible as being on fire, and scholars think that the reference to the burning bush in Deuteronomy, in particular, is a copyist's error, and was originally a reference to Sinai.

Now once Moses came close to investigate the miraculous fire, God called out to him. Moses responded, according to scripture, in which I whole-heartedly believe, and said, "Here am I"; verse 4 of chapter 3, as found in Exodus. This reply, which shows trust and availability, was the same response that Abraham gave when the Lord asked him to sacrifice Isaac (Genesis 22:1, 11).

The Lord asked Moses to take off his sandals, as an act that showed respect and submission. I want you to understand this significant point about the "burning bush" also. The flame of fire in the lowly desert bush, the emblem of Deity and Humanity of Christ and the great name

"I Am" proceeding out from the fire revealed this Almighty Power of Moses from God. If it's done in the flesh, it will consume the person, i.e., "the bush"; however, if it's done by the Power of the Holy Spirit, the bush will burn and not be consumed. So whatever you do in word or in deed, do it as unto the Lord.

Look at that voice, you know, the one that said, "Moses, Moses," it was the very same Voice that said, Martha, Martha." Nothing can be more interesting or instructive than the mode in which the Lord is pleased to reveal Himself to Moses.

So now let's re-picture the scene, if you will, In many parts of the world, people still remove their footwear before entering a house because they don not want to dirty the house of a respected host. Similarly, Moses was entering the house of the Lord, a piece of ground God had chosen to inhabit. The ground was holy because God was there at that time.

Besides revealing His holiness to Moses, God also revealed His faithfulness. Mentioning Abraham, Isaac, and Jacob brought to mind the covenant God had made with these men. God still honored that covenant and would rescue His people because of it. At this point Moses knew that he was talking with God Himself and hid his face out of shame and fear. But just as the bush was not destroyed, neither was Moses consumed by the Lord's presence. Besides being holy, God is also merciful and full of grace.

We have to remember that wherever God is, that place is Holy. And it is Holy only as long as God is there. So "*houses of God*" per se, it's only a Holy House if God abides in it, otherwise it is no longer holy when God is absent. As far as we know, this appearance by God to Moses was the first appearance since Jacob's going down into Egypt about 215 years before. As well, if it is to be noticed, the Lord didn't say, "I was' the God of Abraham ..." etc., but "I am' ..., proving that these Patriarchs were still alive, even though they had died physically a long time before.)

Do you now see and understand that Egypt was a type of the world; "the Lord delivers us from this present evil world"; he does so by the means of the Cross (Galatians 1:4). The Lord delivers us from something, sin, and thereby to something, Salvation, typified by Canaanland. While Egypt represents the world, these various tribes which then occupied the Promised Land typify "flesh" which endeavors to hinder the Believer. All victory is won by and through Christ and the Cross.)

THE COMMISSION

Matthew Henry's Commentary says these words, "As the poorest of the oppressed are not below God's cognizance, so the highest and greatest of their oppressors are not above His check, but He will surely visit for these things."

Do you see how with one man, the Lord would deliver nearly 3 million of His people out of the mightiest nation on Earth, which was determined to hold them captive. It is the same in this present day. All the Lord needs is one man, or woman, who will be willing to preach His Word, and deliverance will be effected, even for the hardest cases. Why? Because God is able to do exceedingly and abundantly above all that we are able to think.

It is my hope that we will learn that the carnal mind is not subject to the Law of God, neither indeed can be. The very Moses, who in 2:11-13 stepped forward with energy to champion his people, is the very same Moses, who in 3:11 steps back and declares himself unequal to the task. Faith neither steps forward nor backward, but holds the Hand which says: *"Certainly I will be with you"*.

I find out within myself, when commissioned to do something, that the human heart is full of questions. Consequently it reasons and questions when unhesitating obedience is that which is due to God; and still more marvelous is the Grace that bears with all the reasonings and answers all the questions. To the Israelites, God had been known by titles, such as "El" or "Elohim," which meand "The Lofty One; or "Shaddai," which means "The Powerful"/ or "Javeh"or Jehovah," : The Existent One." However, these names were more descriptions than anything else.

So here's where we are liken unto the Israelites. God may not have responded as quickly to the Hebrews' cries as they would have like, but He was concerned with their struggles. Because of what He saw in Egypt, He came down to Mount Horeb to speak to Moses and to rescue His people. The Lord spoke with compassion for His people, even mentioning their mistreatment and cries for help. He knew their "sorrows" (Exodus 3:7) and was listening to their pleas for deliverance.

God's plans was to lead the people out of their suffering and slavery to a "spacious", but abundant land, large enough for six nations to live in, where they would enjoy freedom and His generous provision. God, not Moses, would deliver them. But God's plan of action included Moses. He would go to Egypt, confront Pharaoh, and lead the Hebrews out of Egypt. Here's comes Moses' "conflict in route to his destiny".

The task seemed impossible to Moses, but God promised that He would be with him. Moses did not have to fear because it was ultimately the Lord who was saving His people. As a sigh of His pledge to Moses, God promised that when Moses and the people left Egypt, they would serve Him together at that very mountain.

WHAT TO DO WHEN IT SEEMS TO LATE

What do you do when it seems to late? Well I have a few verses of scripture that can help through that period of your life. Donnie McClurkin says, "Yes, after you've done all you can. You just stand. Tell me, how do you handle ... After you've done all you can. You just stand. The words to this marvelous song is provided below. I would like you to not only read them, but let them set and soak into you spirit so that you won't move before God tell you to.

What do you do
When you've done all you can
And it seems like it's never enough?
And what do you say when your friends turn away
And you're all alone?
Tell me, what do you give
When you're given your all and
Seems like you can't make it through?
Well, you just STAND
When there's nothing left to do
You just STAND
Watch the LORD see you through

Yes, after you've done all you can
You just STAND
Tell me, how do you handle
The guilt of your past?
Tell me, how do you deal with the shame?
And how can you smile while your heart has been
broken and filled with pain?
Tell me, what do give when you've given all
Seems like you can't make it through?
You just STAND
When there's nothing left to do
You just STAND
Watch the LORD see you through
Yes, after you've done all you can
You just STAND
You just STAND and
Be not entangled in that bondage again
You just STAND and endure
GOD has a purpose, yes, GOD HAS A PLAN
Hold on, just be strong - GOD will step in
You just STAND!

This song today is as equally important to us as it was when the Lord had to remind Israel that He is the same One Who spoke to the Patriarchs and said, that I have a name that is above every name. For I am called "I AM THAT I AM" and My name shall be Forever. He has to remind them as well as us that He changes not; He is the same yesterday, and today, and forever. His Name is Jesus; and that is God's greatest Name!

We need to understand that God sees everything that is done to His Children, be it negative or positive. Unlike when Moses had made the plans to kill the Egyptian unnoticed,; they didn't succeed, but God now makes the plans, and they are guaranteed of success. This is why this next verse of scripture points to each one of us.

Hebrews 10:36

36 For ye have need of patience, that, after ye have done the will of God, ye might receive the promise.

Listen to what Matthew Poole's Commentary says concerning this verse of scripture. For ye have need of patience: for shows this to be an enforcement of the former direction: Cast not away your confidence, for you have need of grace, which that must maintain in order to carry back your reward. It is therefore absolutely necessary, as well as useful to you, for the bearing of your burdens, persevering in all duty, and waiting for your reward, notwithstanding your reproaches, afflictions, and fiery trials, that you preserve your confidence in maintaining this patience, Hebrews 6:12; Romans 2:7; James 1:4.

That, after ye have done the will of God; that having believed God's promises, obeyed his precepts, endured his trials, and persevered in all, according to the good, acceptable, and perfect will of God; and so exercised our patience, and evidenced our confidence, and finished our work; ye might receive the promise; you may carry back, as your full prize, after your race. It is a necessary and true reportation from God, after his will is done, 1Peter 1:9; 5:4; the reward promised metonymically expressed by the promise, Hebrews 6:15; 9:15; all that life and glorious inheritance in the reality and fullness of it, called a crown of glory that fadeth not away, 1Timothy 4:8; 2Timothy 1:1.

How many times have you looked back on some personal trials in your life and thought, I can't help but to think of "Jarius" of the bible. He came to the Lord with what was probably the greatest and most urgent need of his life. His daughter was dying, but if they hurried, Jesus could save her. As they, his servants or family started for Jarius' house, a woman with a serious nee, but not critical need, jumped ahead of Jesus and Jarius.

I can only imagine what Jairus must have been feeling and thinking: Lord, don't you realize how important this is? This woman is sick, but my daughter is dying. But what seemed like an unnecessary delay was simply an opportunity to reveal the power of God.

There have been times in my life that I have cried out to God in desperation, pleading with Him to answer me, only to arrive at church and hear someone giving testimony of how the Lord provided something they wanted. At that point, I was not rejoicing because they were blessed; I was angry because I was not blessed, or so I thought. I am convinced now that God was working all things together for my good.

God is not bound by the constraints of time and the circumstances we may try to put on Him. Instead, He sees a larger picture and works in our lives to satisfy our deepest needs and desires. When we keep looking to Him, trusting even when it seems He's too late, in time we can feel contentment and joy that is deeper than we ever could have imagined.

We need to understand that God knows and He cares. While he was in Pharaoh's palace, Moses may have believed he could lead his people out of bondage. But 40 years in the desert had likely convinced him that God had abandoned him and his people. How do you act when you're going through you "*desert experience*".

Remember, time and circumstance can wear away our trust in God. However, as someone has said, "Never doubt in the darkness what God has shown you in the light". Today, in the light of God's Word, we see the truth that God is concerned for those who struggle, and He desires to rescue them.

Chapter 4

God's Plan for Moses

It will be easier for you, the reader to understand this next chapter if I identify what a plan is. Merriam Webster's Online dictionary defines plan as a drawing or diagram drawn on a plane. It also states that it is as a top or horizontal view of an object b: a large-scale map of a small area: a method for achieving an end b: an often customary method of doing something : procedure c: a detailed formulation of a program of action d: goal, aim: an orderly arrangement of parts of an overall design or objective or a detailed program.

How many times do we ask God to show us His method for us to achieve the goal that He has for our life; then we begin to make excuses and complain about not being qualified to do it. This is what Moses did in the fourth chapter of Exodus. He's not unlike many of us who do the same thing today, when we are commissioned by God to do a certain task.

How ironic it is for me to be discussing the fourth chapter of Exodus and beginning the fourth chapter of this book at the same time. As you study the fourth chapter of Exodus, beginning at the 10th verse, you'll find these words.

Exodus 4:10-16

10And Moses said unto the LORD, O my Lord, I *am* not eloquent, neither heretofore, nor since thou hast spoken unto thy servant: but I *am* slow of speech, and of a slow tongue.

11 And the LORD said unto him, Who hath made man's mouth? or who maketh the dumb, or deaf, or the seeing, or the blind? have not I the LORD?

12 Now therefore go, and I will be with thy mouth, and teach thee what thou shalt say.

13 And he said, O my Lord, send, I pray thee, by the hand *of him whom* thou wilt send.

14 And the anger of the LORD was kindled against Moses, and he said, *Is* not Aaron the Levite thy brother? I know that he can speak well. And also, behold, he cometh forth to meet thee: and when he seeth thee, he will be glad in his heart.

15 And thou shalt speak unto him, and put words in his mouth: and I will be with thy mouth, and with his mouth, and will teach you what ye shall do.

16 And he shall be thy spokesman unto the people: and he shall be, *even* he shall be to thee instead of a mouth, and thou shalt be to him instead of God.

Because God has given us a greater revelation or example of what He is willing to do for us based on His inspirationally written Word, we should be unlike Moses in this since. We have more examples given to us than did Moses concerning the "Goodness of God". We know that God is not a man that he should lie, neither is He the Son of Man that He should repent. Plainly stated, "God can't lie". If He said He'll do it, then He'll bring it to pass. Listen to what Romans 8: 28-30 promises to us that are willing to follow God's plan.

Romans 8:28-30

28 We know that in everything God works for good with those who love him, who are called according to his purpose.

29 For those whom he foreknew he also predestined to be conformed to the image of his Son, in order that he might be the first-born among many brethren.

30 And those whom he predestined he also called; and those whom he called he also justified; and those whom he justified he also glorified.

Before this become effective in our lives some conditions have to be met. The first condition is that it has to be for "His Purpose" and not ours, which is the second condition; otherwise, all things will not work together for our good.

Please don't forget that it is never the person that is predestined, but rather the Plan that Jesus uses. Also don't forget or get it twisted as my mother would say, concerning verse 29. This doesn't mean that Jesus was Born-Again as a sinner, as some teach but rather that He is the Father of the Salvation Plan, having paid the price on the Cross, which made it all possible.

I again want to refer to Matthew Poole's commentary on verse 30. Listen to what he says in reference to this verse. He hath already given them the beginning and pledge thereof in grace; and will in due time bring them to the possession of eternal life and glory. Some, under this term of glorification would have sanctification included; because, otherwise, they think there is a great defect in this chain of salvation, here set down by the apostle, of which sanctification is one special link; but this is rather to be couched and included in effectual calling, which is the third link, and already spoken of.

Now we are to see that when the people of God are set free from the compulsion of self-exaltation and self-justification and self-preservation, so that we live for the eternal good of other people, then we become the light of the world and the salt of the earth, and people notice in us the reality of God and give him glory (Matthew 5:14-16). Therefore if God's purpose for us is to be accomplished in the world—to make known his glory through lives of love—then we must find a weapon with which to conquer the pride and insecurity that feeds our need to exalt ourselves and justify ourselves and preserve ourselves with postures and poses and performances and prosperity.

OUR WEAPON AGAINST PRIDE AND INSECURITY

The weapon that God has put into the hands of his people is the promise of Romans 8:28. "We know that all things work together for good for those who love God, to those who are called according to his purpose" (KJV). The heart-felt confidence that God Almighty causes everything that happens to me to be good for me is the sword that severs the root of self-exaltation and self-justification and self-preservation. As verse 31 says, "If God is for us, who is against us?"

If, by the sheer grace of his sovereign will, God has taken your side, and works all the pain and pleasure together for your good, then no opponent can really succeed against you. So why exalt yourself? Why justify yourself? Why fret about preserving yourself? If the Lord of the universe has sworn to work for you, why are you anxious about what others think? Why are you all caught up in seeking comfort and security? Your Father knows what you need and he works everything for your good.

We are to leave our exaltation and justification and preservation in his sovereign hands and live in freedom for others. When God's chosen people really believe Romans 8:28, from measles to the mortuary, they are the freest and strongest and most generous people in the world. If Romans 8:28 is that powerful in daily life, then its foundation is utterly practical. Romans 8:29-30 is that foundation. The better we understand it and the more deeply we believe it, the more assured we will be of Romans 8:28. And that will make us a very strong and loving people—to the glory of God!

GOD'S CALLING AND PREDESTINATION

Today our focus is on the first sentence in verse 30: "And those whom he predestined he also called." Last Sunday we zeroed in on the meaning of our "call" and the meaning of "predestination." Today I want to focus on the connection between these two. But first let's sum up our conclusions from last week.

CALLED ACCORDING TO HIS PURPOSE

Romans 8:28 says that all things work together for the good of those who "are called according to his purpose." What does it mean to be called? It means that God has overcome the rebellion of our hearts and drawn us to Christ and created faith and love where there was once a heart of stone. The call is effectual. It creates what it commands. It is not like, "Here Blackie! Here Blackie!" It is like, "Lazarus, come forth!" or, "Let there be light!" The call happens in the preaching of the Word of God by the power of the Spirit of God. It overcomes all resistance and produces the faith that justifies.

One of the key evidences for this truth was the sentence here in verse 30: "those whom he called he also justified." Only people with faith are justified. But Paul says that the called are justified. So the call must in some sense guarantee the faith. Indeed! The call is the creation of the faith. Therefore all who are called are indeed justified.

CALLED ON THE BASIS OF HIS PREDESTINATION

The other thing we saw last week was that this call is not somehow a response to anything we have done. Verse 28 says we are called "according to his purpose." His purpose and plan is the basis of our call, not our purpose or plan. This purpose is described in verse 29. Notice at the beginning of verse 30 that our call is based on our predestination: "those whom he predestined he also called." So the phrase "called according to God's purpose" in verse 28 is virtually the same as called on the basis of God's predestination in verse 30. His predestining and his purposing are the same.

And its content is given in verse 29: "Whom he foreknew he also predestined to be conformed to the image of his Son, in order that he might be the first-born among many brethren." The purpose for which we are predestined is to share the glory of the preeminent Son of God. This purpose or predestination is traced back finally to an act of foreknowing: "Whom he foreknew he also predestined."

So what exactly is predestination based on? Just because people have their different views of what predestination is or isn't does not mean that God bases his predestination on our self-determined faith which he knows ahead of time. That interpretation is intended to preserve the self-determination of the human will. But we have already seen that faith is produced by the call of God not by an act of human self-determination.

Instead what we saw was that there are many other texts to show that when God foreknows, he sets his favor upon or acknowledges or chooses.

So the meaning of verse 29 is that "whom God freely chose, or whom God freely set his favor upon, he also predestined to be like his Son, and whom he predestined, he called." So the call of God is based on God's act of predestination which is in turn based on the election or choice that God makes without any respect to our distinctives at all.

There is a basis for a "Rock-Solid Confidence in the Promise from God" . The practical upshot of this last week was this: if God has chosen you before the foundation of the world apart from any merit or distinctives in you, and has appointed for you a destiny of glorious Christlikeness, and to bring about that purpose has called you by creating faith toward Christ and love toward God, and thus qualified you for the promise of Romans 8:28, then is not your confidence in this promise far greater than if it simply rested on something as wavering and uncertain as your will and decision? "Called according to his purpose" is the great ground of confidence that Romans 8:28 is really true for us.

Today I want us to dwell on the truth that our call is based on God's predestination. Verse 30: "Those whom he predestined, he also called." Our call, our conversion, our regeneration, and the gift of our faith are based on God's eternal election and predestination not on our self-determination.

There are other New Testament texts which say the same thing. One way I can show you this is for you to listen to this next few paragraphs. The way I would like for us to dwell on this is to look at other texts in the New Testament which say this same thing so that we will see how broad the foundation of our confidence in Romans 8:28 really is in God's Word.

In Romans 11:4-8, Paul recalls how Elijah once thought he was the only true believer left, just like some thought God has rejected his people in Paul's day.

> But what is God's reply to him? "I have kept for
> myself seven thousand men who have not bowed
> the knee to Baal." So too at the present time there
> is a remnant, chosen by grace [literally: a remnant
> according to the election of grace]. But if it is by
> grace, it is no longer on the basis of works; otherwise
> grace would no longer be grace. What then? Israel
> failed to obtain what it sought. The elect obtained it
> but the rest were hardened, as it is written, "God gave
> them a spirit of stupor, eyes that should not see and
> ears that should not hear, down to this very day."

Note: Just as God had worked to keep for himself a group of true believers in Elijah's day, so he has in Paul's day. And Paul calls it a remnant "according to the election of grace."

The fact that there is a group of people who believe, are born again, converted, and called, accords with an act of gracious election. Election is the basis of the believing remnant, not vice versa. It does not say that God elected according to who believed, as though election were based on foreknown faith. No. Verse 5: "At the present time there is a remnant, according to the election of grace." The calling into existence of a remnant of true believers accords with God's purpose of election. "Those whom he predestined he also called."

2 Timothy 1:8-9

> Do not be ashamed then of testifying to our Lord, nor
> of me his prisoner, but take your share of suffering
> for the gospel in the power of God, who saved us
> and called us with a holy calling, not in virtue of our
> works but in virtue of his own purpose and the grace
> which he gave us in Christ Jesus ages ago.

Again Paul says that the call is not owing to our deeds. It is owing to God's purpose. Verse 9: "He saved us and called us with a holy calling, not according to our works but according to his own purpose and grace." Our call rests on his purpose, not ours. And the grace of this purpose was "given to us in Christ ages ago." Our call is based on God's eternal election. "Those whom he predestined he also called."

2 Thessalonians 2:13

> But we are bound to give thanks to God always for you, brethren, beloved by the Lord, because God chose you from the beginning to be saved through sanctification by the Spirit and belief in the truth.

It does not say that God chose them on the basis of their foreseen faith. It says the opposite: God chose them with a view to saving them by the work of the Spirit and by faith. The self-determined faith of man does not give rise to God's election. On the contrary. Election gives rise to faith. "Those whom he predestined he also called."

Ephesians 2:4-6

> But God, who is rich in mercy, out of the great love with which he loved us, even when we were dead through our trespasses, made us alive together with Christ (by grace you have been saved), and raised us up with him, and made us sit with him in the heavenly places in Christ Jesus.

You may ask, Where do you see election and predestination in this text? The answer is that I see it in the word love. But you ask, Does not God love everyone? The answer is that he does not love all people in the same way. The love mentioned here is not the universal love that moves God to give life and breath and sunshine and rain. O no, it is far more precious than that.

Paul says, out of THIS love God made us alive when we were dead. Now, if God loved everyone with that love, all people would be made alive in Christ and all would be saved. When Paul gloried in the love of God for him in Jesus Christ, he did not glory merely in the OFFER of salvation to all who would come to Christ. He gloried in the deeper and more wonderful truth that God had brought him to Christ. Once he was dead in sin.

Now he is alive. And the source of this miracle is the love of God. And since God does not perform this quickening for everyone, it is an electing love. And therefore election is indeed in this passage and it is the basis of our conversion, our regeneration, and our faith. "Those whom he predestined he also called."

1 Corinthians 1:26-30

> For consider your call, brethren; not many of you were wise according to worldly standards, not many were powerful, not many were of noble birth; but God chose what is foolish in the world to shame the wise, God chose what is weak in the world to shame the strong, God chose what is low and despised in the world, even things that are not, to bring to nothing things that are, so that no human being might boast in the presence of God. He is the source of your life in Christ Jesus [literally: "of him are you in Christ Jesus; NASB: "by his doing you are in Christ Jesus"], whom God made our wisdom, our righteousness and sanctification and redemption; therefore, as it is written, "Let him who boasts, boast of the Lord."

Consider your call. That is, look around you in Corinth and see what sort of people have become Christians. Consider who has been effectually called to faith. What do you see? Not many wise or powerful or high-born. Why not? Because God is the one who is choosing who will be saved in Corinth, and God intends to choose in a way that will sever the root of all self-exaltation. Three times Paul says, "God chose."

God does not leave the affair of salvation to the self-determination of man because then we would determine the make-up of the church and we would have something to boast in.

Verse 30 says literally, "From him, that is, from God, are you in Christ Jesus." We did not put ourselves in Christ Jesus. God worked in us so that we would be united to Christ in faith. Why? So that no one might boast before God. Therefore let him who boasts boast in the Lord! God made the choices in Corinth. And on the basis of these choices he called, that is, he grafted people into Christ. "Those whom he predestined he also called."

Acts 13:47-48

Paul was preaching in the synagogue in Antioch of Pisidia. When the sermon is over, Luke makes a comment that shows us his deep theological harmony with the apostle's own writings. Paul closes his presentation with these words:

> "For so the Lord has commanded us, saying, 'I have
> set you to be a light for the Gentiles, that you may
> bring salvation to the uttermost parts of the earth.'"
> And when the Gentiles heard this, they were glad
> and glorified the word of God; and as many as were
> ordained to eternal life believed.

This is virtually identical to what Paul says in Romans 8:30. "Those whom he predestined he also called," means the same as, "As many as were (fore-)ordained to eternal life believed." Paul's doctrine of predestination did not in the least deter him from his frontier missionary labor. On the contrary, it spurred him on to know that God had many people among the nations whom he would effectually call in the preaching of the gospel (Acts 18:10). Those whom God has predestined he will most certainly call. Therein lies the hope and confidence of the entire missionary enterprise.

John 8:46-47; 10:25-27

Jesus repeatedly poses the question in John's gospel why some people believe on him and others don't. Never does he give the popular answer that it is owing to the human power of self-determination. He traces it back again and again to something deeper.

> Which of you convicts me of sin? If I tell the truth,
> why do you not believe me? He who is of God hears
> the words of God; the reason why you do not hear
> them is that you are not of God. (8:46-47)

Whether a person is willing to hear and believe the Word of God is owing to something deeper. Is the person OF GOD or not OF GOD? That is, is the person chosen of God? Born of God? Called of God? As many as are "of God" will be willing to hear. As many as are ordained to eternal life believe. "Those whom he predestined he also called."

> The works that I do in my Father's name, they bear
> witness to me; but you do not believe, because you do
> not belong to my sheep. My sheep hear my voice, and
> I know them, and they follow me. (10:25b-27)

"You do not believe because you do not belong to my sheep." Notice it does not say, "You do not belong to my sheep because you do not believe." My belonging to Jesus' sheep is not based on my faith. I must believe in order to give evidence that I belong to Jesus' sheep. And if I persist in unbelief, then I most certainly do not belong to Jesus' sheep.

But my faith did not make me a sheep. God made me a sheep according to the election of grace which he gave me in Christ Jesus ages ago. And when sheep hear the gospel, they believe. Those whom he predestined to be sheep, he also effectually called to faith!

CONCLUSION

The conclusion I draw, then, is that there is a broad foundation in the New Testament for the truth of Romans 8:30, that the call of God is based on his prior predestination, and that this predestination is not based on anything in us: not on our worth as persons (since then everyone would qualify) nor on our faith (which is a gift of God). Our election is unconditional. Our predestination is unconditional. And our effectual calling is unconditional. Whom he foreknew he also predestined and whom he predestined he also called.

The sovereignty of God in salvation strengthens the true security of the believer. If you believe that God has chosen you from all eternity, and that he predestined you to share the glory of his Son, and that he then worked miraculously to call you out of death into life and made you to believe in Christ, then your confidence is simply tremendous that he is for you and will complete the work of your salvation which he planned ages ago.

But if you only believe that God designed a general way of salvation with no particular persons in view, and that it is finally up to you whether you are going to be a part of this salvation or not, then your security will rest on a much weaker foundation. I count it a very precious thing to have been told by God that my eternal life is rooted in his personal, eternal decision to give me a share in the glory of his Son and that my very faith is part of his omnipotent effort to accomplish that purpose for me. What greater security can there be!

Chapter 5

Get Rid of the Excuses

So, because I came to the conclusion that there is a broad foundation in the New Testament for the truth of Romans 8:30, that the call of God is based on His prior predestination, and that this predestination is not based on anything in us: not on our worth as persons (since then everyone would qualify) nor on our faith (which is a gift of God). Our election is unconditional. Our predestination is unconditional. And our effectual calling is unconditional. Whom he foreknew he also predestined and whom he predestined he also called.

It's for that reason and that reason alone, I can say to myself and Moses, "Get Rid of the Excuses". There is a difference between having a valid reason verses having an excuse. But before we go there let's look at some quotes concerning "excuses".

Alexander Pope: Quotes: Excuses
An excuse is worse than a lie, for an excuse is a lie, guarded.

Thomas Fuller: Quotes: Excuses
Bad excuses are worse than none.

Unknown Author: Quotes: Excuses

Don't make excuses, make good.
Publilius Syrus: Quotes: Excuses
Every vice has its excuse ready.

Can you find yourself anywhere within those four quotes. If so, you should analyze your way of thinking and always refer back to Romans 8:28-30. In this chapter I will be getting back to Moses response to his call from God, but I want to take a moment to see if you can find yourself somewhere within this chapter, let alone this book. I found this next tid bit of information on the internet, written by John Funk. Take a close gander at what he says in his article entitled "Excuses, Excuses".

Excuses, Excuses

Recently I had a conversation with a two people who professed to believe in God and who supposedly wanted to have some relationship with God but refused to frequent a church because of "all of the hypocrites who attended." They had nothing but criticism and contempt for people they thought did not live a righteous life but who professed to be Christians. This criticism seems to be a common complaint (or excuse) for those who fail to attend church or fellowship with other believers.

The charge of hypocrisy has been around for a long time. What exactly is hypocrisy? According to Webster's Dictionary, it means "simulation; feigning to be what one is not; or dissimulation; a concealment of one's real character or motives.

More generally, hypocrisy is simulation, or the assuming of a false appearance of virtue or religion; a deceitful show of good character, in morals or religion; a counterfeiting of religion." Looking at the definition, it is clear that hypocrisy has a lot to do with the intent of the person. It applies to a person who intentionally conceals their real character or who deceitfully acts like they possess good moral character when they actually do not.

Jesus Christ Himself confronted hypocrisy during His day on numerous occasions. When He confronted hypocrisy, He attempted to teach a lesson. In the "do not" verses that follow, Christ was teaching

46

about rewards and the value of the act or gift. Notice the commonality contained within those verses.

Matthew 6:2 (NIV)
2 "So when you give to the needy, <u>do not announce it</u> with trumpets, <u>as the hypocrites do</u> in the synagogues and on the streets, to be honored by men. <u>I tell you the truth, they have received their reward in full.</u>

Matthew 6:5 (NIV)
5 "And when you pray, <u>do not be like the hypocrites,</u> for they love to pray standing in the synagogues and on the street corners to be seen by men. <u>I tell you the truth, they have received their reward in full.</u>

Matthew 6:16 (NIV)

16 "When you fast, <u>do not look somber as the hypocrites do,</u> for they disfigure their faces to show men they are fasting. <u>I tell you the truth, they have received their reward in full.</u>

In Matthew 6:2 Christ was addressing a religious act and the way in which that act was administered. Gifts were not to be announced in order to be honored by men; otherwise, the donor of the gift had received his "reward in full." In other words the honor given by men would be all that the donor would ever receive as a gift given in this manner would not be honored by God.

It is fairly common in our society for people to make charitable gifts and some people give very large charitable gifts. There are a number of people who establish charitable trusts or foundations for the purpose of benefiting organizations or the less fortunate. Many of these charitable organizations are well-known and have had a major impact on their donees. The question that arises however is "What is the primary motivation for the making of the gift?" Is it purely for the charitable purpose? Is it because the donor wants to be recognized for their generosity? Is it for creative tax planning purposes?

In Matthew 6:5 and Matthew 6:16 Christ was referring to religious acts which dealt with public demonstrations of the act. Prayer was being offered in public (synagogues and street corners) for the wrong reasons. These individuals wanted to be seen by men. Why would they want to do such a thing? The reason, of course, was to show their contemporaries just how righteous and holy they were. They did not pray in public for the purpose of witnessing to the masses. Rather, it was a "feigning to be what one was not." It was a simulation of the act. There was no desire to commune with God. The underlying desire was to be seen by men.

Similarly, disfigurement of the face was a way of showing that one was undergoing the right of fasting. Fasting was a denial of self in order to grow closer to God. However, the idea of fasting in public was abhorrent to Christ not because of the actual act of fasting but rather because of the intent of the individual. In this instance, just as was the case with public prayer, the intent of the hypocrite was to be seen by his fellow man so that all would know just how godly this individual was. The intent was not to deny oneself but rather it was to glorify oneself.

In each of these verses as like the verses herein below, the term "hypocrites" is used. According to Strong's Greek-Hebrew Dictionary, that word from the Hebrew means "an actor under an assumed character (stage-player), i.e. (figuratively) a dissembler ("hypocrite")." It was an actor, someone acting out a part. It was not someone who was real or genuine but rather someone who was in fact disingenuous. Like Webster's said, it was someone pretending to be someone or something they were not.

Christ went on to deal with hypocrisy in His "woe to you" verses. In each of these verses, Christ specifically addressed the religious leaders of His day, i.e. the teachers of the law (scribes) and the Pharisees. Woe was a primary expression of grief meaning "alas." In each of these verses Christ was criticizing and condemning these leaders for their actions which did nothing to further the Kingdom of God. The fact of the matter was that the religious leaders of His day acted in such a manner that was contrary to God's wishes.

13 "Woe to you, teachers of the law and Pharisees, you hypocrites! You shut the kingdom of heaven in men's faces. You yourselves do not enter, nor will you let those enter who are trying to. Matthew 23:13 (NIV)

15 "<u>Woe to you, teachers of the law and Pharisees, you hypocrites</u>! You travel over land and sea to win a single convert, and when he becomes one, you make him twice as much a son of hell as you are. Matthew 23:15 (NIV)

23 "<u>Woe to you, teachers of the law and Pharisees, you hypocrites</u>! You give a tenth of your spices-mint, dill and cummin. But you have neglected the more important matters of the law-justice, mercy and faithfulness. You should have practiced the latter, without neglecting the former. Matthew 23:23 (NIV)

25 "<u>Woe to you, teachers of the law and Pharisees, you hypocrites</u>! You clean the outside of the cup and dish, but inside they are full of greed and self-indulgence. Matthew 23:25 (NIV)

27 "<u>Woe to you, teachers of the law and Pharisees, you hypocrites</u>! You are like whitewashed tombs, which look beautiful on the outside but on the inside are full of dead men's bones and everything unclean. Matthew 23:27 (NIV)

29 "<u>Woe to you, teachers of the law and Pharisees, you hypocrites</u>! You build tombs for the prophets and decorate the graves of the righteous. Matthew 23:29 (NIV)

In each instance Christ publicly labeled these people as counterfeit, fake, disingenuous and deceitful. Then He specifically told them why He identified them in that way that He did. With all of their rules and regulations, they purposefully shut door to the Kingdom of God to seekers even though they themselves were not going to be allowed to enter; He accused them of chasing down converts only to turn them into something as bad as they were; He accused them of fulfilling the minor requirements of the law while at the same time neglecting the more important aspects of the law such as justice, mercy and faithfulness; He looked inside each of them and criticized them for their motives; He identified their character labeling them filthy and defiled; and finally, He accused them of murder. It is no wonder that they ultimately planned and carried out his execution.

At the end of the Olivet Discourse in the form of an allegory, Christ infers what happens to hypocrites when He speaks about the difference in treatment for those people who are prepared for his rapture of the church and for people who will be unprepared.

Matt 24:45-51 (NIV)

45 "Who then is the faithful and wise servant, whom the master has put in charge of the servants in his household to give them their food at the proper time?

46 It will be good for that servant whose master finds him doing so when he returns.

47 I tell you the truth, he will put him in charge of all his possessions.

48 But suppose that servant is wicked and says to himself, 'My master is staying away a long time,'

49 and he then begins to beat his fellow servants and to eat and drink with drunkards.

50 <u>The master of that servant will come on a day when he does not expect him and at an hour he is not aware of.</u>

51 <u>He will cut him to pieces and assign him a place with the hypocrites, where there will be weeping and gnashing of teeth.</u>

The unprepared will be cut to pieces and assigned a place with the hypocrites where there will be great distress and mourning. Hypocrites are evidently consigned to Hades and ultimately would be consigned to hell (Gehenna).

But some may ask, "What about those Christians who are hypocrites? Are they going to hell?" Those aren't the questions to ask. The question to ask is "Is a hypocritical person truly a Christian?" I submit to you that they are not for the reason that as we have seen already, a hypocrite is somebody pretending to be someone or something they are not. They are deceitful. They are merely actors playing the part.

Their true intention is not to live the life of a Christian but rather to cloak themselves with the cover of Christianity while they carry out their own nefarious schemes. They believe that the claim of Christianity can supply them with credibility that they are other wise lacking.

Getting back to the comments made at the beginning of this article by the two people who refuse to go to church due to perceived hypocrisy, are they right? Is the church filled with hypocrites? Prior to researching and writing this article, I would have told you, "yes, the church is filled with hypocrites; they are just saved hypocrites." Today, my view has changed.

I believe that the church is filled with sinners, people who struggle in their Christian walk every day. However, I no longer believe that the church is filled with hypocrites, i.e. deceitful people who are just play-acting for their own benefit and the benefit of those around them. Yes, there are hypocrites in the church just as there are hypocrites in every walk of life. We encounter disingenuous people virtually everyday; however, do these morally bankrupt people fill the pews on Sunday? I submit to you that by and large they do not. The ones who come aren't fooling anyone. People know.

Moreover, the issue of perceived hypocrisy within the church is a red herring. The simple fact is that you can find a Bible-teaching church that fits you if you will just look around. The world is not filled with churches that are attended exclusively by hypocrites. Hypocrites do not peruse the papers each Saturday picking out the church that they will attend the following day. The refusal of a person to worship God corporately and fellowship with other believers is just that – a refusal.

The New Testament, particularly the Book of Acts, is replete with references concerning the gathering of God's people together.

Acts 2:44-47 (NIV)

44 <u>All the believers were together</u> and had everything in common.

45 Selling their possessions and goods, they gave to anyone as he had need.

46 <u>Every day they continued to meet together</u> in the temple courts. <u>They broke bread in their homes and ate together</u> with glad and sincere hearts,

47 praising God and enjoying the favor of all the people. And the Lord added to their number daily those who were being saved.

1 Corinthians 14:26 (NIV)

26 What then shall we say, brothers? <u>When you come together</u>, everyone has a hymn, or a word of instruction, a revelation, a tongue or an interpretation. All of these must be done for the strengthening of the church.

Ephesians 2:21-22 (NIV)

21 In him <u>the whole building is joined together</u> and rises to become a holy temple in the Lord.

22 And in him <u>you too are being built together</u> to become a dwelling in which God lives by his Spirit.
Ephesians 4:16 (NIV)

16 From him <u>the whole body, joined and held together</u> by every supporting ligament, grows and builds itself up in love, as each part does its work.

It is clear from these verses that the purpose behind the gathering together is to build up the body of believers. When people come together according to God's purpose, it is to edify, support and strengthen their fellow members.

As time grows short and the advent of the Rapture comes closer, the gathering together of God's people becomes more and more important. As we read the news each day, we see gloom and despair spreading throughout God's creation. People, even Christian people, begin to lose hope. There is a way to prevent this loss of hope during these end times.

Hebrews 10:25 (NIV)

25 Let us not give up meeting together, as some are in the habit of doing, but let us encourage one another-and all the more as you see the Day approaching.

So what excuse do you think will be a ticket winner when the Lord says, "Depart from me ye worker of iniquity, I never knew you. How about these excuses or statements exemplifying an excuse, that follow.

Why Go To Church?

Every Sunday many people go to church while others are sleeping or engaged in other weekend activities. Since our weekends are limited, should we spend part of it in church? Let's look at some of the popular reasons for not going first.

EXCUSE: CHURCH IS BORING.

"It is repetitious, predictable and a meaningless ritual. I would rather sleep in. I work hard all week and I deserve it!"

Answer: Church is repetitious but so is life. The days of our lives are structured around cycles of work, eating, family and recreation times. Any of these activities can become boring if we don't strive to find something interesting or enjoyable about them. Sunday mornings at church are a time to make new friends and renew old ones; to learn about the Bible and share problems as well as to thank God for another week of life.

The objective in going to church is to seek to build our relationship with God and others. Many people go to church to fulfill an obligation through some ritual and so are reduced to actions without meaning.

Church worship is all about an encounter with God and others that changes who we are. Not going to church on a Sunday morning because you deserve a sleep-in does not explain why you miss church on Saturday or Sunday night. The problem is much deeper than the time of the day - it is a matter of selfishness.

EXCUSE: WHY BOTHER GOING TO CHURCH WHEN ALL THEY WANT IS MONEY!?

Answer: If you choose to get involved in any kind of group, be it the PTA, Boy Scouts or whatever, it will cost you in time and money. It is true that, if you don't get involved in anything, you will have maximum control of your time and money. However, you will miss friendships and opportunities to be a good influence in the lives of others. Each of us decides where to spend our time and money. Each of us will either invest it in some purpose or waste it on the pleasures of the moment. Jesus said that there is an eternal investment that will not fade, rust or decay when we do good works that show our love for God and others (Matthew 6:19-20).

Ponder this! You do not control your life. You cannot guarantee that you will be alive the next week, day, hour or moment. Human life is a gift from God and He controls the measure of it (Psalm 139:16). Our intelligence, talents and appearance are largely determined by genetics (which is to say by God who made us individually unique). Therefore, who we are, when and where we are born, how long we live, etc., are all gifts from God. Is it unreasonable for God to ask for a portion of it to acknowledge Him and His sovereignty? Did you like those and do think you can get by with those when Jesus Christ returns? I know not. Take the time and read the aforementioned excuses and the responses given to those excuses, and maybe you'll have a change of heart. At least, I pray you will.

This chapter is so good to me, that I thought I'd leave the best for last. I preached a sermon on "No more excuses", so I thought I'd leave you with a few more excuses; as quoted by others.

Only man who is really free is the one who can turn down an invitation to dinner without giving an excuse. ~Jules Renard

Excuses are the nails used to build a house of failure. ~Don Wilder and Bill Rechin

Don't make excuses - make good. ~Elbert Hubbard

He who excuses himself accuses himself. ~Gabriel Meurier, *Trésor des sentences* Several excuses are always less convincing than one. ~Aldous Huxley, *Point Counter Point*

Maybe you don't like your job, maybe you didn't get enough sleep, well nobody likes their job, nobody got enough sleep. Maybe you just had the worst day of your life, but you know, there's no escape, there's no excuse, so just suck up and be nice. ~Ani Difranco

How strange to use "You only live once" as an excuse to throw it away. ~Bill Copeland

Don't do what you'll have to find an excuse for. ~Proverb

No one ever excused his way to success. ~Dave Del Dotto

Excuses are the tools with which persons with no purpose in view build for themselves great monuments of nothing. ~Steven Grayhm

And oftentimes excusing of a fault

Doth make the fault the worse by the excuse.

~William Shakespeare

Bad excuses are worse than none. ~Thomas Fuller

A lie is an excuse guarded. ~Jonathan Swift

Hold yourself responsible for a higher standard than anyone else expects of you. Never excuse yourself. ~Henry Ward Beecher

If you don't want to do something, one excuse is as good as another. ~Yiddish Proverb

We excuse our sloth under the pretext of difficulty. ~Marcus Fabius Quintilian

Whoever wants to be a judge of human nature should study people's excuses. ~Hebbel

We have more ability than will power, and it is often an excuse to ourselves that we imagine that things are impossible. ~François de la Rochefoucauld

Two wrongs don't make a right, but they make a good excuse. ~Thomas Szasz, *The Second Sin*

Difficulty is the excuse history never accepts. ~Edward R. Murrow

Pessimism is an excuse for not trying and a guarantee to a personal failure. ~Bill Clinton

We weave our excuses around events.

Thin, poor quality cloth of justification

Poor substitutes for the heavy tribal blankets

Once we wove to wrap our children.

~Phillip Pulfrey, "Cloth," *Beyond Me*, www.originals.net

Destiny: A tyrant's authority for crime and a fool's excuse for failure. ~Ambrose Bierce

Every vice has its excuse ready. ~Publilius Syrus

We are all manufacturers - some make good, others make trouble, and still others make excuses. ~Author Unknown

One of the most important tasks of a manager is to eliminate his people's excuses for failure. ~Robert Townsend

Success is a tale of obstacles overcome, and for every obstacle overcome, an excuse not used. ~Robert Brault, www.robertbrault.com

Your letter of excuses has arrived. I receive the letter but do not admit the excuses except in courtesy, as when a man treads on your toes and begs your pardon - the pardon is granted, but the joint aches, especially if there is a corn upon it. ~Lord Byron

Bad men excuse their faults; good men abandon them. ~Author Unknown

He that is good for making excuses is seldom good for anything else. ~Benjamin Franklin

It is wise to direct your anger towards problems - not people, to focus your energies on answers - not excuses. ~William Arthur Ward

Any excuse will serve a tyrant. ~Aesop

We have forty million reasons for failure, but not a single excuse. ~Rudyard Kipling

The person who really wants to do something finds a way; the other person finds an excuse. ~Author Unknown

Justifying a fault doubles it. ~French Proverb

The best day of your life is the one on which you decide your life is your own. No apologies or excuses. No one to lean on, rely on, or blame. The gift is yours - it is an amazing journey - and you alone are responsible for the quality of it. This is the day your life really begins. ~Bob Moawad

Conflict En Route to Destiny

The absent are never without fault, nor the present without excuse. ~Benjamin Franklin

Usually, terrible things that are done with the excuse that progress requires them are not really progress at all, but just terrible things. ~Russell Baker

Sometimes I wish I had a terrible childhood, so that at least I'd have an excuse. ~Jimmy Fallon

Never ruin an apology with an excuse. ~Kimberly Johnson

I hope you enjoyed this chapter enough to not use any of these excuses. Whatever God has called you do, believe me, He has already equipped you to succeed. You just have to take Him at His Word. So I guess we'll get back to Moses and his desire to make excuses for not being the one who God needs.

57

Chapter 6

Equipped For the Task

We ended the last chapter in a funny sort of way. I didn't pick on Moses until now. The last chapter offered many thoughts on numerous excuses, but it all still goes back to God. What He said you can do, you can do. But listen to brother Moses in Exodus 4:10-17 via the Amplified version.

Exodus 4:10-17

10 And Moses said to the Lord, O Lord, I am not eloquent {or} a man of words, neither before nor since You have spoken to Your servant; for I am slow of speech and have a heavy {and} awkward tongue.

11 And the Lord said to him, Who has made man's mouth? Or who makes the dumb, or the deaf, or the seeing, or the blind? Is it not I, the Lord?

12 Now therefore go, and I will be with your mouth and will teach you what you shall say.

13 And he said, Oh, my Lord, I pray You, send by the hand of [some

other] whom You will [send].

14 Then the anger of the Lord blazed against Moses; He said, Is there not Aaron your brother, the Levite? I know he can speak well. Also, he is coming out to meet you, and when he sees you, he will be overjoyed.

15 You must speak to him and put the words in his mouth; and I will be with your mouth and with his mouth and will teach you what you shall do.

16 He shall speak for you to the people, acting as a mouthpiece for you, and you shall be as God to him.

17 And you shall take this rod in your hand with which you shall work the signs [that prove I sent you].

We are to see here, how in verses 10-17, Moses continued backward to the work God designed him for; there was much of cowardice, slothfulness, and unbelief in him. We must not judge of men by the readiness of their discourse. A great deal of wisdom and true worth may be with a slow tongue.

God sometimes makes choice of those as his messengers, who have the least of the advantages of art or nature, that his grace in them may appear the more glorious. Christ's disciples were no orators, till the Holy Spirit made them such. God condescends to answer the excuse of Moses.

Even self-diffidence, when it hinders us from duty, or clogs us in duty, is very displeasing to the Lord. But while we blame Moses for shrinking from this dangerous service, let us ask our own hearts if we are not neglecting duties more easy, and less perilous. The tongue of Aaron, with the head and heart of Moses, would make one completely fit for this errand. God promises, I will be with thy mouth, and with his mouth. Even Aaron, who could speak well, yet could not speak to purpose, unless God gave constant teaching and help; for without the constant aid of Divine grace, the best gifts will fail.

In this chapter, Moses is our example of someone who was reluctant to accept the responsibilities God was giving him. God, however, assured Moses that He would provide the means to carry out all the duties related to the position. All Moses needed to do was to accept God's call and then show up ready to do God's bidding.

Moses had "more excuses than a barrel of monkeys" for not accepting the leading position, as it pertained to leading the Israel out of Egypt. Listen to the excuses that Moses tried to use. I am nobody important (Exodus 3:11), I don't know what to tell the Israelites (3:13); and the Israelites might not believe me (Exodus 4:1). Then when we turn back to this passage of scriptures, he argued that he was a poor speaker. And when God dealt with that objection (as He had dealt with all the others), Moses simply said (in effect), "I don't want to go. Send somebody else!" No wonder God was angry with him.

But, even in His anger, God made it clear that He had a plan, and that He wasn't going to abandon that plan just because Moses was uncooperative. Does that sound like you, when God has called you to a particular task that seemed to hard for you to do? Is anything to hard for the Lord, in you to do? I know not.

Instead, God revealed His plan in verses 14b-16: He would send Aaron, Moses' older brother, to help Moses carry out His instructions. Just as God would use Moses as a "mouthpiece," so Moses could use Aaron as a "mouthpiece." Moses and Aaron would have to accept the responsibilities God was assigning to them, and God would accept the responsibility for making the plan effective.

As I go to the next verses of scripture (Exodus 4:27-31), I want you to remember that the Bible doesn't always record events in the order in which they happened. All we need to know is that it indeed happened as the Bible describes. For example, in verse 14, the Lord told Moses that Aaron was already on his way to meet him. But verse 27 records how the Lord told Aaron to go, so verse 27 would have to come before verse 14 if the story were told in chronological order.

What a joyful time it must have been for Moses and Aaron to see one another after 40 years of separation! Their emotions must have been intensified even further by the fact that they both knew that this reunion had been arranged by God Himself. But it wasn't just a chance for long-separated brothers to enjoy each other's fellowship. There was important work to do. God had told Aaron to go meet Moses, but He hadn't told him the purpose of the meeting. Moses had to explain that to Aaron. Moses performed the miraculous signs for his brother and "taught him how to do them; verse 30 says that it was Aaron, not Moses, who performed the signs before the people once they were back in Egypt.

Everything went according to God's plan. Moses and Aaron accepted the responsibilities God had given them and communicated God's message to the people as He had instructed them to do. The people believed and praised God in anticipation of His intervention to free them from slavery. At the end of chapter 4, everything seems to be going well.

WHO'S IN CHARGEDI

How would you like to be the one who has to go and tell President Obama, the Lord said, "thus and such". That would be a huge task to do, wouldn't it? Especially since you know the President has so many body guards and secret service agents at his disposal. Not to mention, all the U. S. Armed Forces members awaiting his beckoning call. This is just an up to date version of what Moses had to do back then. We, like Moses have to remember, "who's in charge".

After Moses and Aaron explained to the Israelites that the Lord was preparing to free from their slavery to the Egyptians, the next move was for Moses and Aaron to speak to Pharaoh (the king of Egypt) and request permission for the people to leave Egypt peacefully. The dialogue that ensued had all the marks of a typical Middle Eastern political (or economic) negotiation. Even today, tourists in that part of the world enjoy "haggling" with vendors over the terms of a sale, much as Westerners do when buying and selling real estate, automobiles and other high-priced items. This particular negotiation didn't go very well.

First, Moses and Aaron told Pharaoh that the Lord was commanding him to let the Israelites go so that they could hold a religious festival in the uninhabited land in what is nowadays called the Sinai Peninsula. Pharaoh responded with scorn; he had no intention of taking orders from any "God" that wasn't one of his gods, and he definitely rejected the idea of letting the Israelites leave Egypt.

In the next "round" Moses and Aaron explained to Pharaoh that the Israelite' God had appeared to them, and they "toned down" their request from a command to a plea, adding that they were concerned that the Israelites might suffer disease or violence if they were to fail to offer sacrifices as they had been instructed to. But Pharaoh completely ignored this suggestion and alleged that the whole subject was intended as a diversion. He spoke to Moses and Aaron as if they, themselves, were slaves (rather than national leaders), and ordered those who were in charge of the labor force to make the work even more difficult, so that the people would have less free time (as if they had much as it was)!

"WHY ME, LORD?"

Moses like many other heroes of the Bible, responded to the apparent failure of his first efforts at "negotiating with Pharaoh by resorting to prayer. He brought his complaint to God, obeying God's instructions had not (at least, not yet) achieved the promised result; in fact, the situation had worsened considerably. Moses even dared to lay the blame for this fact on God, accusing God of failing to keep His promises.

Moses was neither the first nor the last of God's prophets to blame God for the misfortunes that he experienced. The Bible portrays God as bearing the ultimate responsibility for everything that happens, good or bad (Isaiah 45:7).

Furthermore, those who spoke harshly to God for the way He manages the universe (such as Moses did in Exodus 5:22-23) are seldom rebuked for doing so. God can take the criticism and He is usually very gracious about it. But woe to the man who blames God for something He, Himself, had done. That is what arouses God's anger. The message is clear: we should accept responsibility for our own actions, and allow God to take the responsibility for everything else that happens to us.

The Lord could have responded angrily to Moses' complaint if He had wanted to; instead, He graciously ignored the prophet's whining and simply reiterated His promise to intervene on the Israelites behalf. "Hang in there, Moses!" He seemed to be saying. "The best is yet to come!"

What the Lord had in mind (He told Moses) was the demonstration of such awesome power (in the 10 plagues) that Pharaoh would not merely let the Israelites go, but actually drive them out of Egypt. In the process, Pharaoh would learn to whom the true authority belonged; God, not Pharaoh. Pharaoh would end up both knowing the Lord and letting Israel go, in direct contrast to what he had said in Exodus 5:2.

Now we're coming to first part of Moses "Conflict Enroute to his destiny". So here we are getting ready to "Cross the Red Sea". Here's what Exodus 14:15-22 states:

15 And the LORD said unto Moses, Wherefore criest thou unto me? speak unto the children of Israel, that they go forward:

16 But lift thou up thy rod, and stretch out thine hand over the sea, and divide it: and the children of Israel shall go on dry ground through the midst of the sea.

17 And I, behold, I will harden the hearts of the Egyptians, and they shall follow them: and I will get me honour upon Pharaoh, and upon all his host, upon his chariots, and upon his horsemen.

18 And the Egyptians shall know that I am the LORD, when I have gotten me honour upon Pharaoh, upon his chariots, and upon his horsemen.

19 And the angel of God, which went before the camp of Israel, removed and went behind them; and the pillar of the cloud went from before their face, and stood behind them:

20 And it came between the camp of the Egyptians and the camp of Israel; and it was a cloud and darkness to them, but it gave light by night to these: so that the one came not near the other all the night.

21And Moses stretched out his hand over the sea; and the LORD caused the sea to go back by a strong east wind all that night, and made the sea dry land, and the waters were divided.

22 And the children of Israel went into the midst of the sea upon the dry ground: and the waters were a wall unto them on their right hand, and on their left.

Here we will see where God will give His greatest direction to Israel's leader.

First, what he must do himself. He must, for the present, leave off praying, and apply himself to his business (Exodus 14:15): Wherefore cryest thou unto me? Moses, though he was assured of a good issue to the present distress, yet did not neglect prayer. We read not of one word he said in prayer, but he lifted up to God his heart, the language of which God well understood and took notice of. Moses' silent prayers of faith prevailed more with God than Israel's loud outcries of fear, (Exodus 14:10).

Note:
1. Praying, if of the right kind, is crying to God, which denotes it to be the language both of a natural and of an importunate desire.

2. To quicken his diligence, Moses had something else to do besides praying; he was to command the hosts of Israel, and it was now a requisite that he should be at his post.

Secondly, what he must order Israel to do. He was to speak to them, that they go forward. Some think that Moses had prayed, not so much for their deliverance (he was assured of that)as for the pardon of their murmurings, and that God's ordering them to go forward was an intimation of the pardon. There is no going forward with any comfort but in the sense of our reconciliation to God. Moses had bidden them stand still, and expect orders form God; and now orders are given. They thought they must have been directed either to the right hand or to the left. "No," says God, "speak to them to go forward, directly to the sea-side;" as if there had lain a fleet of transport-ships ready for them to embark in.

Note: When we are in the way of our duty, though we met with difficulties, we must go forward, and not stand in mute astonishment; we must mind present work and then leave the even to God, use means and trust him with the issue.

Finally, what he might expect God to do. Let the children of Israel go as far as they can upon dry ground, and then God will divide the sea, and open a passage for them through it, (Exodus 14:16-18). God designs, not only to deliver the Israelites, but to destroy the Egyptians; and the plan of his counsels is accordingly.

1. He will show favor to Israel; the waters shall be divided for them to pass through (Exodus 14:16). The same power could have congealed the waters for them to pas over; but Infinite Wisdom chose rather to divide the waters for them to pass through; for that way of salvation is always pitched upon which is most humbling. Thus it said, with reference to this (Isaiah 63:13-14), He led them through the deep, as a beast goes down into the valley, and thus made himself a glorious name.

2. He will get him honor upon Pharaoh. If the due rent of honor be not paid to the great landlord, by and from whom we have and hold our beings and comforts, he will distrain for it, and recover it. God will be a loser by no man. In order to this, it is threatened: I, behold I, will harden Pharaoh's heart, (Exodus 14:17). The manner of expression is observable: I, behold I, will do it. "I that may do it;" so it is the language of His sovereignty. We may not contribute to the hardening of any man's heart, not withhold any thing that we can do towards the softening of it; but God's grace is his own, he hath mercy on whom he will have mercy, and whom he will be hardeneth. "I, that can do it;" so it is the language of his power; none but the Almighty can make the heart soft (Job 23:16), nor can any other being make it hard." I, that will do it;" for it is the language of His justice; it is a righteous thing with God to put those under the impressions of His wrath who have long resisted the influences of His grace. It is spoken in a way of triumph over this obstinate and presumptuous rebel" "I even , will take an effectual course to humble him; he shall break that would not bend." It is an expression like that (Isaiah 1:24),

Ah, I will ease me of my adversaries.

A guard set upon Israel's camp where it now lay most exposed, which was in the rear, Exodus 14:19-20. The angel of God, whose ministry was made use of in the pillar of cloud and fire, went from before the camp of Israel, where they did not now need a guide (there was no danger of missing their way through the sea, nor needed they any other word of command than to go forward), and it came behind them, where now they needed a guard (the Egyptians being just ready to seize the hindmost of them), and so was a wall of partition between them.

There it was of use to the Israelites, not only to protect them, but to light them through the sea, and, at the same time, it confounded the Egyptians, so that they lost sight of their prey just when they were ready to lay hand on it. The word and providence of God have a black and dark side towards sin and sinners, but a bright and pleasant side towards those that are Israelites indeed. That which is a savour of life unto life to some is a savour of death unto death to others.

This was not the first time that he who in the beginning divided between light and darkness (Genesis 1:4), and still forms both (Isaiah 45:7), had, at the same time, allotted darkness to the Egyptians and light to the Israelites, a specimen of the endless distinction which will be made between the inheritance of the saints in light and that utter darkness which for ever will be made between the inheritance of the saints in light and that utter darkness which for ever will be the portion of hypocrites. God will separate between the precious and the vile. This concludes the first part of Moses' and Aaron's "***Conflict Enroute to Destiny***". The Bible will give you the conclusion of the whole matter; from start to finish. Please read it daily, for it offers direction for your journey to God.

Chapter 7

Experiencing God, While Facing Conflict En route to Destiny

I want to thank the Lord first for all that He has taken me through, in this life, and all that He allowed me to experience as a member of "Mount Zion Missionary Baptist Church, Hinesville, Georgia, where the pastor is Reverend M. L. Jackson. It was this bible study lesson entitled, "Experiencing God: Facing Conflict En route to Destiny" that prompted me to do a sermon on this lesson text. I have yet to preach this particular sermon, but I have able to witness to a fellow yokes man in the gospel, by the name of Pastor Tommie Means, New Bethel Christian Church. This lesson was lesson 14, from the Bible Study guide, Wednesday, April 9, 2006; I'll never forget it.

Here are the study scriptures used: Mark 11:1-11; Matthew 21:1-11; Luke 19:28-40 and John 12:12-29. The lesson scriptures come from Luke 19:28-40 and St. John 12:12-19. In this lesson the question is asked, "Can conflict prevent you from reaching your destiny? It follows up with a second question, "Why or why not?" My answer to that question is a definitive yes, if you take your eyes off of God, while your conflicting stage of life. Ask me how I know. I am a personal witness as to someone who got off track because of the conflict presented to me in my lifetime. As I wrote that last sentence, the Holy Spirit gives a resounding "No". It says to me, "Not when God is in Charge". That is the difference when you answer from the fleshly mind as it is compared to a spiritual mind. Conflicting isn't it. Don't be dismayed it happens to us all, but greater is He that is in us, than he that is in the world.

The introduction of the lesson reminded us that many people have different reactions to revelation. Read what the lesson says and see if you can picture in your mind what the words are speaking to your "spirit". Some in the crowds reacted to the revelation of Christ, with a thirst to see more acts of the miraculous; Judas, one of Jesus' disciples who walked daily with Jesus, reacted with pure selfishness; Mary's reaction to the revelation of Jesus Christ's pending death was sacrifice and worship.

Our revelation of Jesus Christ, by the Holy Spirit, brings us to and understanding that regardless of conflict, trouble and disillusionment, our faith in Jesus Christ will encourage us to head to our destiny. Philippians 1:6 records, we are confident of this very thing; He who has begun a good work in us will perform and perfect it until the day of Jesus Christ. Let's take a moment to look at that verse of scripture.

So, Brother Matthew Henry, what do you have to say concerning this verse of scripture? He states that the apostle proceeds after the inscription and benediction to thanksgiving for the saints at Phillipi. He tells them what it was he thanked God for, upon their account. I need you to observe what he says here.

THE APOSTLE'S THANKFULNESS AND JOY

First, Paul remembered them: he bore them much in his thoughts; and though they were out of sight, and he was at a distance from them, yet they were not out of his mind: or, Upon every mention of you, ep pase te mneia. As he often thought of them, so he often spoke of them, and delighted to hear them spoken of. The very mention of them was grateful to him: it is a pleasure to hear of the welfare of an absent friend. How many of us really think that way of each other; especially of other saints of the "Household of Faith"? Do we really take time to make mention or be happy because of a brother or sister being mentioned in our presence? Or are we just glad not to hear about them at all? How sad a commentary, if that be the case!!! In Paul's case though, it was different. He was glad to hear about absent friends, what about you?

Secondly, he remembered them with joy. At Philippi he was maltreated; there he was scourged and put into the stocks, and for the present saw little of the fruit of his labor; and yet he remembers Philippi with joy. He looked upon his sufferings for Christ as his credit, his comfort, his crown, and was pleased at every mention of the place where he suffered. So far was he from being ashamed of them, or loath to hear of the scene of his sufferings, that he remembered with joy. I I can learn from Paul in this situation. I am just the opposite. I don't want to hear anything concerning my sufferings or maltreatment, as it pertains to Hinesville, Georgia. I need God to help me, even as I write this chapter, to deliver me from my inward feelings concerning Mount Zion Baptist Church, Pastor M. L. Jackson and those who looked down on me because I did what most humans do, fall from following God the way that I needed to do. What I do remember, concerning Mt Zion and Pastor Jackson, is some to the last words he said to me, *"a lot of folks won't be glad to see you back"*. Whether that was true or not, as a friend and pastor, he shouldn't have said it to me; one of his ministers in whom he had ordained. I have to call him and ask him to forgive me for what I feel towards him, and not what he feels about me. Help me Lord with this task. Amen.

Thirdly, Paul remembered them in prayer: Always in every prayer of mine for you all, Philippians 1:4. The best remembrance of our friends is to remember them at the throne of grace. Paul was much in prayer for his friends, for all his friends, for these particularly. It should seem, by this manner of expression, that he mentioned at the throne of grace the several churches he was interested in and concerned for particularly and by name. He had seasons of prayer for the church at Philippi. God gives us leave to be thus free with Him, though, for our comfort, he knows whom we mean when we do not name them.

Fourthly, he thanked God upon every joyful remembrance of them. Observe, Thanksgiving must have a part in every prayer; and whatsoever is the matter of our rejoicing ought to be the matter of our thanksgiving. What we have the comfort of, God must have the glory of. He thanked God, as well as made requests with joy. As holy joy is the heart and soul of thankful praise, so thankful praise is the lip and language of holy joy.

And the last thing to remember is, as in our prayers, so in our thanksgiving, we must eye God as our God: I thank my God. It encourages us in prayer, and enlarges the heart in praise, to see every mercy coming from the hand of God as our God. *"I thank my God upon every remembrance of you"*. We must thank our God for others' grace and comforts, and gifts and usefulness, as we receive the benefit of them, and God receives glory by them.

But what is the matter of this thanksgiving? He gives thanks to God for the comfort he had in them: for your fellowship in the gospel, from the first day until now, Philippians 1:5. Also, observe that the Gospel fellowship is a good fellowship; and the meanest Christians have fellowship in the gospel with the greatest apostles, for the gospel salvation is a common salvation (Jude 1:3), and they obtain like precious faith with them, 2 Peter 1:1. Those who sincerely receive and embrace the gospel have fellowship in it form the very first day: a new-born Christian, if he is true new-born, is interested in all the promises and privileges of the gospel from the first day of his becoming such; until now.

Observe this, it is a great comfort to ministers when those who begin well hold on and persevere. Some, by their fellowship in the gospel, understand their liberality towards propagation the gospel, and translate **kinonia**, not communion, but communication. But, comparing it with Paul's thanksgiving on the account of other churches, it rather seems to be taken more generally for the fellowship which they had, in faith, and hope, and holy love, with all good Christians; a fellowship in gospel promises, ordinances, privileges, and hopes; and this from the first day until now.

For the confidence he had concerning them (Philippians 1:6): Being confident of this very thing, &c. Observe, the confidence of Christians is the great comfort of Christians, and we may fetch matter of praise from our hopes as well as from our joys; we must give thanks not only for what we have in our present possession and evidence of, but for what we have the future prospect of. Paul speaks with much confidence concerning the good estate of others, hoping well concerning them in the judgment of charity, and being confident in the judgment of faith that if they were sincere they would be happy: "That he who has begun a good work in you will perform it unto the day of Jesus Christ. A good work among you, **en hymin**, so it may be read: understand it, in the general, of the planting of the church among them.

He who hath planted Christianity in the world will preserve it as long as the world stands. Christ will have a church till the mystery of God shall be finished and the mystical body completed. The church is built upon a rock, and the gates of hell shall not prevail against it. But it is rather to be applied to particular persons, and then it speaks of the certain accomplishment of the work of grace wherever it is begun.

Lastly, there are six things that I would like to bring to your attention concerning Paul and what he is offering us.

1. The work of grace is a good work, a blessed work; for it makes us good, and is an earnest o good to us. It makes us like God, and fits us for the enjoyment of God. That may well be called a good work which does us the greatest good.

2. Wherever this good work is begun it is of God's beginning; He has begun a good work in you. We could not begin it ourselves, for we are by nature dead in trespasses and sins: and what can dead men do towards raising themselves to life; or how can they begin to act till they are enlivened in the same respect in which they are said to be dead? It is God who quickens those who are thus dead, Ephesians 2:1; Colossians 2:13.

3. The work of grace is but begun in this life; it is not finished here; as long as we are in this imperfect state there is something more to be done.

4. If the same God who begins the good work did not undertake the carrying on and finishing of it, it would lie for ever unfinished. He must perform it who began it.

5. We may be confident, or well persuaded, that God not only will not forsake, but that he will finish and crown the work of His own hands. For, as for God, His work is perfect.

6. The work of grace will never be perfected till the day of Jesus Christ, the day of His appearance. When he shall come to

judge the world, and finish His mediation, then this work will be complete, and the top-stone will be brought forth with shouting. We have the same expression, Philippians 1:10.

As we study further, this lesson entitled, "Experiencing God: Facing Conflict En route to Destiny", I need to turn your attention to how Jesus ministers in His humanity. Our Lord ministered in His humanity on the earth for three years. Jesus came with the purpose and destiny in mind. He was well aware of how He would revolutionize the world by His death, burial and resurrection. Christ modeled for us and yet abides in us, the death: dying to the flesh; burial: burying of the old man with his sins; resurrection: rising in newness of the Spirit and empowered to live eternally.

In His ministry on earth, Jesus asked his disciples, **"Who do men say that I, the Son of Man am?" They answered, "Some say John the Baptist, some Elijah, and others Jeremiah or one of the prophets."** Jesus went on to ask his disciples, "But who do you say that I am?" Simon Peter answered and said, "You are the Christ, the Son of the Living God." Jesus answered and said to him, "Blessed are you, Simon Bar Jonah, for flesh and blood has not revealed this to you, but my Father who is in Heaven."

HUMILITY IS KEY TO FULFILLING DESTINY

Humility is the quality or condition of being humble. The term "humility" is derived from the Latin word "humilis", which is translated not only as humble but also alternatively as "low", or "from the earth", and "humus", humid, which in the past it was believed that emotions, diseases, and depressions were caused by imbalances of body waters. Because the concept of humility addresses intrinsic self-worth, it is emphasized in the realm of religious practice and ethics where the notion is often made more precise and extensive. Humility as a religious or spiritual virtue is different from the act of humiliation or shaming though the former may follow as a consequence of the latter.

I'm not a philosopher, but I want you to know what philosophers have to say to the matter of humility being the key to fulfilling destiny. Just for the record I was a "Behavioral Analysis Student" in college, and that's why I wanted you to get a different view on the subject matter in which I will presenting you throughout the rest of this chapter.

Traditionally, faith and reason have each been considered to be sources of justification for belief. Because both can purportedly serve this same epistemic function, it has been a matter of much interest to philosophers and theologians how the two are related and thus how the rational agent should treat claims derived from either source.

Some have held that there can be no conflict between the two, that reason properly employed and faith properly understood will never produce contradictory or competing claims, whereas others have maintained that faith and reason can (or even must) be in genuine contention over certain propositions or methodologies. Those who have taken the latter view disagree as to whether faith or reason ought to prevail when the two are in conflict. Kierkegaard, for instance, prioritizes faith even to the point that it becomes positively irrational, while Locke emphasizes the reasonableness of faith to such an extent that a religious doctrine's irrationality, conflict with itself or with known facts is a sign that it is unsound. Other thinkers have theorized that faith and reason each govern their own separate domains, such that cases of apparent conflict are resolved on the side of faith when the claim in question is, say, a religious or theological claim, but resolved on the side of reason when the disputed claim is, for example, empirical or logical.

Some relatively recent philosophers, most notably the logical positivists, have denied that there is a domain of thought or human existence rightly governed by faith, asserting instead that all meaningful statements and ideas are accessible to thorough rational examination. This has presented a challenge to religious thinkers to explain how an admittedly nonrational or transrational form of language can hold meaningful cognitive content.

This article traces the historical development of thought on the interrelation of faith and reason, beginning with Classical Greek conceptions of mind and religious mythology and continuing through the medieval Christian theologians, the rise of science proper in the early modern period, and the reformulation of the issue as one of 'science versus religion' in the twentieth century. I am going to just introduce to you, through my writing, the introduction of the subject matter entitled "Faith and Reason", as it appears on the "Internet Encyclopedia of Philosophy".

FAITH AND REASON

Faith and reason are both sources of authority upon which beliefs can rest. Reason generally is understood as the principles for a methodological inquiry, whether intellectual, moral, aesthetic, or religious. Thus is it not simply the rules of logical inference or the embodied wisdom of a tradition or authority. Some kind of algorithmic *demonstrability* is ordinarily presupposed.

Once demonstrated, a proposition or claim is ordinarily understood to be justified as true or authoritative. Faith, on the other hand, involves a stance toward some claim that is not, at least presently, demonstrable by reason. Thus faith is a kind of attitude of trust or assent. As such, it is ordinarily understood to involve an act of will or a commitment on the part of the believer. Religious faith involves a belief that makes some kind of either an implicit or explicit reference to a transcendent source. The basis for a person's faith usually is understood to come from the authority of revelation. Revelation is either direct, through some kind of direct infusion, or indirect, usually from the testimony of an other. The religious beliefs that are the objects of faith can thus be divided into those what are in fact strictly demonstrable (*scienta*) and those that inform a believer's virtuous practices (*sapientia*).

Religious faith is of two kinds: evidence-sensitive and evidence-insensitive. The former views faith as closely coordinated with demonstrable truths; the latter more strictly as an act of the will of the religious believer alone. The former includes evidence garnered from the testimony and works of other believers. It is, however, possible to hold a religious belief simply on the basis either of faith alone or of reason alone. Moreover, one can even lack faith in God or deny His existence, but still find solace in the practice of religion.

The basic impetus for the problem of faith and reason comes from the fact that the revelation or set of revelations on which most religions are based is usually described and interpreted in sacred pronouncements, either in an oral tradition or canonical writings, backed by some kind of divine authority. These writings or oral traditions are usually presented in the literary forms of narrative, parable, or discourse. As such, they are in some measure immune from rational critique and evaluation. In fact even the attempt to verify religious beliefs rationally can be seen as a kind of category mistake. Yet most religious traditions allow and even encourage some kind of rational examination of their beliefs.

The key philosophical issue regarding the problem of faith and reason is to work out how the authority of faith and the authority of reason interrelate in the process by which a religious belief is justified or established as true or justified. Four basic models of interaction are possible.

(a) The **conflict model**. Here the aims, objects, or methods of reason and faith seem to be very much the same. Thus when they seem to be saying different things, there is genuine rivalry. This model is thus assumed both by religious fundamentalists, who resolve the rivalry on the side of faith, and scientific naturalists, who resolve it on the side of reason.

(b) The **incompatibilist model**. Here the aims, objects, and methods of reason and faith are understood to be distinct. Compartmentalization of each is possible. Reason aims at empirical truth; religion aims at divine truths. Thus no rivalry exists between them. This model subdivides further into three subdivisions. First, one can hold faith is **transrational**, inasmuch as it is higher than reason. This latter strategy has been employed by some Christian existentialists. Reason can only reconstruct what is already implicit in faith or religious practice. Second, one can hold that religious belief is **irrational**, thus not subject to rational evaluation at all. This is the position taken ordinarily by those who adopt negative theology, the method that assumes that all speculation about God can only arrive at what God is not. The latter subdivision also includes those theories of belief that claim that religious language is only metaphorical in nature. This and other forms of irrationalism result in what is ordinarily considered fideism: the conviction that faith ought not to be subjected to any rational elucidation or justification.

(c) The **weak compatibilist model**. Here it is understood that dialogue is possible between reason and faith, though both maintain distinct realms of evaluation and cogency. For example, the substance of faith can be seen to involve **miracles**; that of reason to involve the scientific method of hypothesis testing. Much of the Reformed model of Christianity adopts this basic model.

(d) The **strong compatibilist model**. Here it is understood that faith and reason have an organic connection, and perhaps even parity. A typical form of strong compatibilism is termed **natural theology**. Articles of faith can be demonstrated by reason, either deductively (from widely shared theological premises) or inductively (from common experiences). It can take one of two forms: either it begins with justified scientific claims and supplements them with valid theological claims unavailable to science, or it starts with typical claims within a theological tradition and refines them by using scientific thinking.

An example of the former would be the cosmological proof for God's existence; an example of the latter would be the argument that science would not be possible unless God's goodness ensured that the world is intelligible. Many, but certainly not all, Roman Catholic philosophers and theologians hold to the possibility of natural theology. Some natural theologians have attempted to unite faith and reason into a comprehensive metaphysical system.

The strong compatibilist model, however, must explain why God chose to reveal Himself at all since we have such access to him through reason alone.

The interplay between reason and faith is an important topic in the philosophy of religion. It is closely related to, but distinct from, several other issues in the philosophy of religion: viz., the existence of God, divine attributes, the problem of evil, divine action in the world, religion and ethics, religious experience and religious language, and the problem of religious pluralism. Moreover, an analysis of the interplay between faith and reason also provides resources for philosophical arguments in other areas such as metaphysics, ontology, and epistemology.

While the issues the interplay between faith and reason addresses are endemic to almost any religious faith, this article will focus primarily on the faith claims found in the three great monotheistic world religions: Judaism, Islam, and particularly Christianity.

This rest of the article will trace out the history of the development of thinking about the relationship between faith and reason in Western philosophy from the classical period of the Greeks through the end of the twentieth century.

With all that being said, it all starts and ends with God and what His Son did on Calvary's Cross. So now I would like you to note the lowliness of Jesus. Most kings expect the people to fully acknowledge their authority and greatness with pomp and pageantry. Most kings do not serve, are not expected to serve and do not expect to be expected to serve. Most kings are not defined by humility, but are more accurately defined by their wealth, opulence, holdings, public approval and inheritance.

- Jesus came to honor our Father

- Jesus came to win the hearts and lives of men for eternity. He did not come to boast of Himself. He did not come demonstrate wealth or royalty.

- For example: king spake and said, Is not this great Babylon, that I have built for the house of the kingdom by the might of my power, and for the honour of my majesty?

One problem with destiny is the thoughts of expectations, followed by or intertwined with prophecy. Look at this scenario, Jesus is and claimed to be the Messiah: The Jews believed in the coming Messiah. They expected him to come as an earthly king, in pageantry, pomp, and circumstance; however Jesus came in humility.

We often do not perceive humility as the steppingstone to destiny. Our expectation is to be exalted, known and publicly approved. We see public approval as the validation that God has ordained and called us into something. Flesh and Spirit are enmity to one another, in other words, God does not approve or validate fleshly ideas, perceptions, and visions of grandeur. If you don't believe it, read 1 Peter 5:7. It reads: **1Peter 5:5-7**

5:5 Likewise, ye younger, submit yourselves unto the elder. Yea, all *of you* be subject one to another, and be clothed with humility: for God resisteth the proud, and giveth grace to the humble.

5:6 Humble yourselves therefore under the mighty hand of God, that he may exalt you in due time:

5:7 Casting all your care upon him; for he careth for you.

So what is these verses saying to us as it pertains to humility and the humility that Jesus Christ demonstrated. Plain and simple, "Humility is Recommended". We see here how the apostle had just settled and explained the duty of pastors and spiritual guides of the church; he now comes to instruct the flock. He starts by instructing themselves on how to behave themselves towards their ministers and to one another.

He starts off calling them the younger, as being younger than their grave pastors, and to put them in mind of their inferiority, the term younger being used by our Savoir to signify and inferior, Luke 22:26. He exhorts those that are younger and inferior to submit themselves to the elder, to give due respect and reverence to their persons, and to yield to their admonitions, reproof, and authority, enjoining and commanding what the word of God requires, Hebrews 13:17.

One reason the "Body of Christ" is having problems of "conflict), while trying to reach their "destiny" is because they haven't grasped or fully grasped what the apostle is saying to them in these verses of scripture. Let' continue on to see what else he is saying to us, "the Body of Christ".

As to one another, the rule is that they should all be subject one to another, so faras to receive the reproofs and counsels one of another, and be ready to bear one another's burdens, and perform all the offices of friendship and charity one to another; and particular persons should submit to the directions of the whole society, Ephesians 5:21; James 5:16.

These duties of submission to superiors in age or office, and subjection to one another, being contrary to the proud nature and selfish interests of men, he advises them to be clothed with humility, . "Let your minds, behavior, garb, and whole frame, be adorned with humility, as the most

beautiful habit you can wear; this will render obedience and duty easy and pleasant; but, if you be disobedient and proud, God will set himself to oppose and crush you; for he resisteth the proud, when he giveth grace to the humble."

I need you to observe some things for my sake and yours.

1. Humility is the great preserver of peace and order in all Christian churches and societies, consequently pride is the great disturber of them, and the cause of most dissensions and breaches in the church.

2. There is a mutual opposition between God and the proud, so the word signifies; they war against him, and he scorns them; he resisteth the proud, because they are like the devil, enemies to himself and to his kingdom among men, Proverbs 3:34.

3. Where God giveth grace to be humble, he will give more grace, more wisdom, faith, holiness, and humility. Hence the apostle adds: Humble yourselves therefore under the mighty hand of God, that he may exalt you in due time, 1 Peter 5:6. "Since God resisteth the proud, but giveth grace to the humble, therefore humble yourselves, not only one to another, but to the great God, whose judgments are coming upon the world, and must begin at the house of God (1 Peter4:17); his hand is almighty, and can easily pull you down if you be proud, or exalt you if you be humble; and it will certainly do it, either in this life, if he sees it best for you, or at the day of general retribution."

Here are some things for all of us to learn, first, learn the consideration of the omnipotent hand of God should make us humble and submissive to him in all that he brings upon us. Secondly, humbling ourselves to God under His hand is the next way to deliverance and exaltation; patience under His chastisements, and submission to His pleasure, repentance, prayer, and hope in his mercy, will engage His help and release in due time, (James 4:7, 10).

The apostle already knew that these Christians were already under very hard circumstances, rightly supposes that what he had foretold of greater hardships yet a coming might excite in them abundance of care and fear about the event of these difficulties, what the issue of them would be a heavy burden, and a sore temptation, he gives them the best advice, and supports it with a strong argument.

His advice is to cast all their care, or all care of themselves, upon God. "Throw your cares, which are so cutting and distracting, which wound your souls and pierce your hearts, upon the wise and gracious providence of God; trust in Him with a firm composed mind, for he careth for you. He is willing to release you of you care, and take the care of you upon himself. He will either avert what you fear, or support you under it. He will order all events to you so as shall convince you of his paternal love and tenderness towards you; and all shall be so ordered that no hurt, but good, shall come unto you, "Matthew 6:25; Psalms 84:11; Romans 8:28".

So we should now see how important humility is to God and should be to us. As we continue looking at Jesus and His humility, we see Jesus deliberately fulfilled the prophecy. Matthew 21:2-3; Christ sent two disciples into the city to borrow a donkey and her young colt. He borrowed the two animals from another man, probably another disciple. It was done as prophesied.

- The man was a believer… he did not ask, "who is the Lord?" The man responded to the request promptly for he was aware that Lord meant "Jehovah".

- The Lord demonstrated His divine ability to activate and orchestrate anything, anywhere and anytime and through HE CHOOSES. God's strength and authority supersedes all others.

- Jesus did not own the donkeys; he borrowed them to fulfill scripture prophecy.

EN ROUTE TO DESTINY - THE COLT WAS BORROWED

I want to present a scripture to you for your reading. Read Zechariah 9:9, as it states the following words:
Zechariah 9:9

9 Rejoice greatly, O daughter of Zion; shout, O daughter of Jerusalem: behold, thy King cometh unto thee: he *is* just, and having salvation; lowly, and riding upon an ass, and upon a colt the foal of an ass.

So look at what's happening here now. Here begins a prophecy of the Messiah, and his kingdom is plain from the literal accomplishment of the Zechariah 9:9 in, and its express application to, Christ's riding in triumph into Jerusalem, (Matthew 21:5; John 12:15).

Within this scripture, a notice is given of the approach of the Messiah promised, as matter of great joy to the Old-Testament church: Behold, thy king cometh unto thee. Christ is a king, invested with regal powers and prerogatives, a sovereign prince, and absolute monarch, having all power both in heaven and on earth. He is Zion's king. God has set Him upon His holy hill of Zion, Psalms 2:6. In Zion his glory as a king shines; thence his law went forth even the word of the Lord.

In the gospel-church his spiritual kingdom is administered; it is by him that the ordinances of the church are instituted, and its officers commissioned; and it is taken under his protection; he fights the church's battles and secures its interests, as its king. "This king has been long in coming, but now, behold, he cometh; he is at the door. There are but a few ages more to run out, and he that shall come will come. He cometh unto thee; the Word will shortly be made flesh, and dwell within thy borders; he will come to his own. And therefore rejoice, rejoice greatly, and shout for joy; look upon it a s good news, and be assured it is true; please thyself to think that he is coming, that he is on his way towards thee; and be ready to go forth to meet him with acclamations of joy, as one not able to conceal it, it is so great, nor ashamed to own it, it is so just; cry Hosanna to him". Christ's approaches ought to be the church's applauses.

This next section of paragraphs will depict Jesus, as He is, amiable in the eyes of all his loving subjects, and his coming to them very acceptable. He is a righteous ruler and all his acts of government will be exactly according to the rules of equity; for He is just. He is a powerful protector to all those that bear faith and true allegiance to him, for he has salvation; treasures of salvation are in Him.

He is servatus, saving Himself (so some read it), rising out of the grave by His own power and so qualifying Himself to be our Savior. He is a meek, humble, tender Father to all His subjects as His children.

81

He is lowly, poor and afflicted (so the word signifies), so it denotes the meanness of his condition. Having emptied Himself, He was despised and rejected of men. But the evangelist translates it so as to express the temper of His spirit. He is meek, not taking state upon Him, nor resenting injuries, but a humbling Himself from first to last, condescending to the mean, compassionate to the miserable. This was a bright and excellent character of Him as a prophet (Matthew 11:29; Learn of me, for I am meek and lowly at heart), and no less so as a king. It was a proof of this that, when He made His public entry into His own city (and it was the only passage of his life that had any thing in it magnificent in the eye of the world), he chose to ride, not upon a stately horse, or in a chariot, as great men used to ride, but upon an ass, a beast of service indeed, but a poor silly and contemptible one, low and slow, and in those days ridden only by the meaner sort of people. It wasn't an ass fit for use, but an ass's colt, a little foolish unmanageable thing, that would be more likely to disgrace his rider that be any credit to him; and that not his own neither, nor helped off, as sometimes a sorry horse is, by good furniture, for he had no saddle, no housings, no trappings, no equipage, but his disciples' clothes thrown upon the colt; for he made himself of no reputation when he visited us in great humility.

Now that Jesus' humility has been made more clearer, we now understand why the "Lord had need of the borrowed "colt". With that being said, there should never be any task thought to be to small in the service of God. The demonstration of riding in on a donkey was a powerful statement of the character and purpose of Jesus Christ. This was God's will prophesied generations before Christ came. God wanted Jesus to proclaim His Messianic position very clearly for people to see. Jesus claimed to be the Messiah, God's very own Son. This is the very thing that angered the Jews to the point of wanting to kill him. God already was fully aware of the hearts and minds of man. The prophecy was deliberately fulfilled. Jesus demonstrated that He could do ministry without owning anything material. Selah (pause and meditate on that). In order to fulfill scripture Jesus rode in on a colt, a borrowed colt. He had purpose and went about to fulfill it contrary to man's expectations.

I've talked about expectations, but do you understand exactly what expectations are? As I give you the definition of expectation, it allows me to set up 2 Corinthians 8:9 for you, in order that you may understand Who Jesus was and just what He did as went on His course to His "Destiny", for us all; that we may live eternally with Him, in Paradise; if we have accepted as Lord, Savior and Master of our lives.

Expectation is a looking forward to or an anticipation of looking for as due, proper, or necessary. It is a thing looked forward to by reason or warrant for looking forward to something; prospect for the future, as of advancement or prosperity the probability of the occurrence, duration, etc. of something, esp. as indicated by statistics.

Now look at what 2 Corinthians 8:9 says simply:

9 For ye know the grace of our Lord Jesus Christ, that, though he was rich, yet for your sakes he became poor, that ye through his poverty might be rich.

Verse 9, seemed to really confuse the issue for most followers of prophecy. Some had expectations of the Messiah coming one way, and others of another. But Jesus came in the humblest way possible, poor. Listen with your mind, "For ye know the grace of our Lord Jesus Christ; calls to mind, the free love of your Lord and Master Jesus Christ, which you know, believing the gospel, which gives you a true account of it, and having in your own souls experienced the blessed effects of it: He was rich, being the Heir of all things, the Lord of the whole creation, Hebrews 1:2, all things were put under his feet.

Yet for sakes he became poor; yet that he might accomplish the work of your redemption, and purchase His Father's love for us, he took upon the form of a servant, stripped himself of his robes of glory, an clothed himself with the rags of flesh, denied himself in the use of his creatures, had not where to lay down his head, was maintained from alms, people ministering to him of their substance.

That ye through his poverty might be rich; and all this that you might be made rich, with the riches of grace and glory; rich in the love of God, and in the habits of Divine grace; which was all effected by his poverty, by his making himself of no reputation, and humbling himself. If after your knowledge of this, by receiving and believing the gospel, and experiencing this, in those riches of spiritual gifts and graces and hopes of glory which you have, you shall yet be bound strait hearted in compassionating the poverty and afflicted state of his poor members, or strait-handed in ministering unto them, how will you in any measure answer this great love, or conform to this great example.

Here are some things that people needed to know concerning their expectations of the "Coming Messiah" and their thoughts on how it was going to go down.

- People had to be warned because what was expected was not going to happen the way it was anticipated

- There is danger in being so fervent in our own ideas that we miss what really happens; Fervent expectation can miss the event when the event occurs a little different than we expect. God is moving and we missed Him because He came differently than we expected.

- Thy King cometh meek' ..... meek and humble not as a reigning monarch

- Thy King cometh sitting on a donkey ..... Not as a conqueror (though He is) riding on a white stallion but as a King of peace on a donkey. He came to save the world through peace, to reconcile the world to the God of love; not the god of hate, war and retaliation. He was not coming to kill the Romans, men or governments, but to reconcile the world to God.

Wow, that alone blew the minds of all those that thought that they had the correct expectation of the "Coming Messiah". But now comes the real "Conflict" to His Destiny. Man's expectations sometimes conflict with the Will of God. It was not time for the kingdom of God to appear (12:11-27). The Jews expected something else. Jesus' approach conflicted with what they expected. Jesus had to come, suffer and die first. The people did not understand that the church age must run its course before the kingdom could come. Jesus' approach into the city resulted in acceptance of His kingly stature. The people received Him as they would receive a King. They shouted Hosanna (God with us) at this time, but later cried "crucify Him". They cried "Son of David" which was the title of the Messiah. They shouted "blessed is He that cometh in the name of the Lord". They shouted, "Hosanna in the Highest" which means "God save, we pray" Thou art the Highest.

So where's the conflict, you ask? Here it is. The people who received Jesus as King that day were willing to accept Him as an earthly King. They were willing to accept what authority and power He would use on their behalf. They believed the Messiah to be the one to come and deliver them from Roman rule. It was about the earthly government for them. The farthest thought form their minds was the spiritual rule and reign over their lives. They wanted the benefits of the earthly rule. Jesus had many, many followers because of this ….. But later there would be none.

Remember, we should worship Him in spirit and in Truth

But Jesus' death on the Cross would defeat all satanic powers; not just unjust government rulers.

Conflict en route to destiny for Jesus:

The Romans sensed that a popular uprising might be coming. The Herodians, who were the Jewish ruling party, feared they would be overthrown. The Pharisees were stirred to deep in anger, envy and hatred toward Jesus, for their traditions and outward righteousness were being condemned by Jesus. The common people were convinced that their day had finally arrived in Jesus of Nazareth.

So, in conclusion, we have a revelation of God through the face of Jesus Christ. He is the Son fo the Living God. Jesus came with the divine purpose, knowing He would face the conflict of changing the minds and hearts of men. He suffered. He came to lay down His life through crucifixion, to be buried and to be resurrected by the Power of God the Father. He knew of His destiny to redeem man to God. He also humbled Himself and was obedient to reach His destiny so we can reach ours in Him. Now the question still remains, **"How will you handle conflict, as God leads you to destiny?"** (06/20/09)

End Notes

The Practice of Facilitation: Managing Group Process and Solving Problems, Quorum Books, Greenwood Publishing, 1998

New International Version (NIV) Copyright © 1973, 1978, 1984 by International Bible Society

The Master Teacher (USPS 535-060) (ISSN 0746-6986) is published quarterly by the R.H. Boyd Company, 6717 Centennial Blvd, Nashville, Tennessee 37209-1017.

Unless otherwise noted, Scripture quotations are from the Holy Bible, New International Version, copyright 1973, 1978, 1978, 1984 by International Bible Society. Used by permission of Zondervan Publishing House.

info@rapturenext.com

Matthew Henry's Whole Bible Commentary
World Bible Publishers Iowa Falls, Iowa

Alston, William. "History of Philosophy of Religion." *The Routledge Encyclopedia of Philosophy.* Vol. 8. Ed. E. Craig. New York: Routledge, 1998. Pp. 238-248. [This article provides a good basic outline of the problem of faith and reason].

Copleston, Frederick. *Medieval Philosophy*. New York: Harper, 1952.

Helm, Paul, ed. *Faith and Reason*. Oxford: Oxford University Press, 1999.[This text has an excellent set of readings and good introductions to each section. Some of the above treatment of the introductions to each period are derived from it].

McGrath, Alister, ed. *The Christian Theology Reader*. Oxford: Basil Blackwell, 1995. [This text provided some of the above material on early Christian philosophers.]

Meagher, Paul, Thomas O'Brien and Consuelo Aherne, eds. *Encyclopedic Dictionary of Religion*. 3 Vols. Washington DC: Corpus Publications, 1979.

Murphy, Nancey. "Religion and Science." *The Routledge Encyclopedia of Philosophy*. Vol. 8. Ed. E. Craig.. New York: Routledge, 1998. Pp. 230-236

Murphy, Nancey. *Theology in the Age of Scientific Reasoning*. Ithaca NY: Cornell University Press, 1990.

Peterson, Michael, William Hasker, Bruce Reichenback, David Basinger. *Philosophy of Religion: Selected Readings*. Oxford: Oxford University Press, 2001. [This text was helpful for the above treatments of Richard Dawkins and Nancey Murphy.]
Plantinga, Alvin. "Religion and Epistemology." *The Routledge Encyclopedia of Philosophy*. Vol. 8. Ed. E. Craig. London/New York: Routledge, 1998. Pp. 209-218.
Pojman, Louis, ed. *Philosophy of Religion: An Anthology*. 2nd ed. Belmont CA.: Wadsworth, 1994. [This text provides a good introduction to the philosophy of religion. Some of the above treatments of Kant, Pascal, Plantinga, Cahn, Leibniz, Flew, Hare, Mitchell, Wittgenstein, and Hick are derived from its summaries].
Pomerleau, Wayne. *Western Philosophies of Religion*. New York, Ardsley House, 1998. [This text serves as the basis for much of the above summaries of Augustine, Aquinas, Descartes, Locke, Leibniz, Hume,

Kant, Hegel, Kierkegaard, James, Wittgenstein, and Hick.]

Rolston, Holmes III. *Science and Religion: A Critical Survey.* New York: Random House, 1987. [This has a good section on the anthropic principle.]

Solomon, Robert, ed. *Existentialism.* New York: The Modern Library, 1974.

Taylor, Charles. *A Catholic Modernity?* Oxford: Oxford University Press, 1999.

Taylor, Charles. *Sources of the Self.* Cambridge MA.: Harvard University Press, 1989.

Wolterstoff, Nicholas. "Faith." *The Routledge Encyclopedia of Philosophy.* Vol. 3. Ed. E. Craig. London: Routledge, 1998. Pp. 538-544. [This text formed the basis for much of the above treatment of "Reformed Epistemology."]